Based on the works of L. Ron Hubbard

Education

FOSTERING REASON AND
SELF-DETERMINISM IN STUDENTS

HERON® BOOKS PUBLISHING

Applied Scholastics International

11755 Riverview Dr.

St. Louis, MO, 63138

USA

appliedscholastics.org

Heron Books, Inc.

20950 SW Rock Creek Road

Sheridan, OR 97378

USA

heronbooks.com

ISBN: 978-0-89739-162-7

Printed in the USA

14 October 2019

To help one progress chapter by chapter, with increasing understanding, confidence and ability to use the information, two free learning guides have been created to accompany this book.

The first is designed for more independent study, while the second requires access to a courseroom and trained supervisor.

Education: Fostering Reason and
Self-Determinism in Students
(for independent study)

Education: Fostering Reason and
Self-Determinism in Students

Get your free learning guides at
heronbooks.com/apsbooks-learningguides

And this I believe:
that the free, exploring mind of the individual
human is the most valuable thing in the world.
And this I would fight for: the freedom of the mind
to take any direction it wishes, undirected.

John Steinbeck, *East of Eden*

Introduction

This book represents a comprehensive collection of L. Ron Hubbard's observations and insights on education, learning and children. In combination with the materials on study technology, these writings form the philosophical underpinnings of a new approach to education, one that fosters reason and self-determinism in students.

The text was prepared from essays, articles, lectures and other excerpts spanning the late 1930s to the early 1980s. Dates for the early lectures and essays comprising Part One are provided to help with context.

In a 1971 lecture, Hubbard said, "Some people go all of their lives looking for the mystery of the pattern of the pyramids and others go looking for the Mayan civilization and how it built things. I go looking for the knowledge people have lost as a primary expeditionary action."

It was in such a spirit that this compilation was done.

We hope our expeditionary efforts help bring you and your students great success and that you in turn join us in ensuring that this knowledge is not lost.

With that, we present *Education: Fostering Reason and Self-Determinism in Students.*

—Editors

Table of Contents

PART TWO
BASIC PRINCIPLES

21 FOR PARENTS

22 SCALES

APPENDIX

PART ONE

Senior Data Early Lectures and Essays

1

Self-Determinism and the Ability to Reason

(1951)

INTRODUCTION

By their very nature basic principles, every time they are examined, tend to become more basic. Critical exploration uncovers simple underlying fundamentals. Yet, in spite of this fact, the tendency of the greater number of people is to complicate a subject in relaying it. Rarely does one try to advance knowledge by making it simple. The usual fate of a new postulate[1] is building it up into something so complicated it would confuse even the original creator of the postulate!

Original thinkers of the stature of Newton, for example, presented their ideas very simply. Newton stated that there are three laws of motion: inertia, interaction and acceleration. In relaying these laws some struggling scientists feel that if everybody understands the information as well as they, their prestige is thereby lowered. Many individuals are upset, evidently, by going "backwards" in a subject toward simplicity, and insist on going "forwards" toward incomprehensible complexity and confusion. This reaching back for earlier simplicities is, however, the direction that any seeker after truth must take. The moment earlier simplicity is reached, complex data falls apart and becomes simple.

Unfortunately, when people have been taught scholastically by authoritarian teaching methods—a mass of facts forced down the student's throat on threat of failing—they find themselves confused when a new fundamental appears because they have to reevaluate everything they know about the subject. It took years to accumulate, memorize and study the ideas they've acquired, and just as it is difficult to coax people to give up some of their possessions, so it is very

---

1 **postulate**: a proposition or idea assumed as true for the purposes of further reasoning. Also, to assume (something) to be true, real or necessary, especially as a basis for reasoning; put something forth.

trying to them to be asked to give up some of their facts and ideas. Robbing a person of money is no more difficult than robbing a person of such a collection of ideas and facts.

A complicated mass of doctrine has made students who have learned it feel important. They have not tried to resolve problems with the newfound knowledge, but have assumed that they know all that is necessary to be known about the subject. A new simplicity is an attack upon this self-assuredness. They will resist.

Thus it is that progress in the field of physics or chemistry is met usually not with acclaim but with suspicion. What is acceptable to people is something within their frame of reference fitting a majority of their facts. Something which puts new facts into the field and removes old facts is usually combated.

In approaching the principles presented here, one should decide what one is trying to do with a student and evaluate all theory in this light. The information is not tender and fragile; it does not have to be approached with the awe and reverence which is demanded in some fields. All the information here, both theory and technique, should be submitted to these tests: Does it help teachers teach? Does it help students learn?

TEACHING STUDENTS TO REASON

So we begin with a simplicity, which is the statement that education can lie along two lines: The first is to give students data. The second is to teach students to reason with the data they have.

Much modern education hardly recognizes the second method—developing the ability to reason in the student. When we ask why a person needs reason, we find that reason is the ability to extrapolate new data from the existing data. Knowing "all there is to know" about a subject is not enough. The individual must have the ability to know, as the necessity arises, the things that are not known by extrapolating them from the data that is known.

There is a difference between memorizing and reasoning. Knowledge is more than data; it is also the ability to draw conclusions.

It takes brilliant reasoning power to be happy in this world. If all children were taught to *reason* as they learned a few facts, they would have what nature intended them to have, a better castle for their defense.

SELF-DETERMINISM DEFINED

In order to discuss reason, we first need to define the word self-determinism.

Self-determinism refers to one's ability to direct oneself. A self-determined person can reason things out and make good decisions about what to do rather than just react. When one is self-determined, one is not merely a puppet dancing on the strings of the environment; one can control oneself or, when appropriate, choose to accept control from another.

As a note, when we say control, we simply mean willingness and ability to start, change and stop one's activities, body and environment. However, you are stating a greater truth when you say that control is *predictable change* because start and stop are necessary to change. You might say the thinking or philosophic definition of control would be predictable change.

We all strive to be as self-determined as possible.

Self-determinism is sometimes confused with refusal to cooperate or willfulness in non-survival directions. There is a difference between self-determinism and what we might call "selfish determination" where an individual acts only in terms of his or her own irrational desires with no broader view. As self-determinism increases, an individual increasingly uses the data available to think about the effects of an action on self and others, reasoning and directing self rationally toward beneficial goals.

SELF-DETERMINISM AND REASON

Reason, the ability to extrapolate, goes hand-in-glove with self-determinism. As soon as individuals feel that they have a right to reason, to extrapolate from data, they will do so. As this right to reason is inhibited, self-determinism is inhibited in direct ratio. As self-determinism is inhibited, not only do they feel they have no right to move where they wish or do what they wish, but they feel that they cannot use the data they observe.

To increase a person's self-determinism is to increase the person's ability to reason. They are almost the same thing.

A student whose self-determinism has markedly improved but who has not learned "all the information" of his or her schooling is a worthy result. A student who has learned "all the information" but experienced a reduction in self-determinism is an unworthy result.

ADAPTING THE ENVIRONMENT VERSUS ADAPTING TO IT

It is unfortunate that many schools of thought propagate the theory that the purpose of human life is to adapt and that the person who does not is maladaptive[2].

Human life does not seem to know that it is supposed to adapt to the environment: it keeps trying to adapt the environment to itself! The quickest way to estimate the survival potential of an individual is by that individual's relationship with the environment: Are they adapting it or adapting to it?

In order to survive, an organism must be more than an object, it must have the force of life in it. It must be a causative agent. Individuals who can reason can change their environment. If they cannot reason, they cannot change their environment.

The better individuals can reason, the better they can improve their survival potential in their own environment. If one wanted to control human beings like animals, or objects, one would only need to convince them that they have no need to use reason, that they only have to adjust to their environment. The essential difference between an object and a successful organism is the ability to reason, the ability to keep the environment under control and adjust the environment to self.

---

2 **maladaptive**: showing inadequate adjustment to the situation or environment.

INTERRUPTION OF SELF-DETERMINISM

Any education which is done on an authoritarian basis is an effort to control and dominate the student. It may succeed in something but not in increasing the ability of the student to reason.

How would one go about destroying the ability to reason? It would be by prohibiting students from reaching their own conclusions. It would be by inhibiting them from acting upon their own data and causing them to act upon arbitrary data which is forced upon them. The result is confusion and indecision, a condition in which the student can be taken control of and directed by another person for that person's own ends. The less self-determined people are, the more they can be controlled against their rational will by others in their vicinity.

In training a dog, a person extends his or her own influence over the dog, and the dog becomes merely an extension of the person. The dog accepts its subordinate and dependent position, its dog's life. A cat or a human being will not accept such a position. A cat is an independent hunter and must make its own decisions. If children are trained in such a way that much of their self-determinism is interrupted, they will not be successful human beings. They will not even be acceptable to the people who were so careful to train them into this apathy.

Human beings cannot be trained successfully like dogs, no matter how many authoritarians there are in the world who think they can be or should be. A human being who is trained in an authoritarian manner will either succumb or retaliate. The trainer will have either a case of complete apathy to deal with or an angry rebel or, worse yet, a covertly hostile rebel.

Human beings have to be reached with reason.

To make people irrational it is only necessary, then, to interrupt their reasoning process and force arbitrary conclusions on them. They are then owned and must be moved and motivated by their "owner" to survive. If not so moved and motivated, once their ability to reason has been interrupted, they will not survive. Parents who train their child this way are training the child *not to survive*.

EMOTIONAL TONE OF EDUCATION

It will be of interest to the educator that education has its own position on the emotional tone scale[3] and will therefore raise and lower an individual in emotional tone.

Education designed to inhibit and restrain, to create conformity in the individual to the social order,[4] has the unfortunate effect of reducing the individual in emotional tone. This would be authoritarian education and would be from antagonism down.

Education which invites and stimulates reason and seeks to accelerate the individual toward a successful and happy level of existence and has enough faith in individuals to assume the good usage of the education, raises the individual in emotional tone.

One can, by reviewing the education of any individual, discover much supportive evidence for this, since it will be found that those subjects in which the individual is able will be those which were taught by methods above the tone of antagonism. And those subjects in which the individual is poor, lacking accuracy or self-determinism and failing in the ability to reason with them, were taught by methods which would be found from antagonism down on the tone scale.

As a society declines, it more and more resorts to authoritarian teaching and attempts increasingly to impress upon individuals that they must adjust to their environment and that they cannot adjust their environment to them. The educational process becomes one of semihypnotically receiving doughy masses of data and regurgitating them upon examination papers. Reason and self-determinism are all but forbidden.

---

3 **emotional tone scale**: (also *tone scale*) a scale of emotional tones (levels) ranging from the highest to the lowest. These are in part: enthusiasm, cheerfulness, conservatism, contented, boredom, antagonism, anger, fear, grief, apathy. This scale can be found in chapter 22.

4 **social order**: the institutions, customs and social structures of a given society, particularly in the sense of protecting and preserving a way of life.

CONCLUSION

Successful living depends basically upon a person's ability to reason. A person's best weapon is knowledge.

Any new discovery or simplification is valid and useful directly in ratio to its enlargement of one's ability to reason with the knowledge one has.

For this increases the person's self-determinism.

And that is the goal.

2

What's Wrong with Modern Education?

(1950)

INTRODUCTION

There is a great deal of talk about the inertia of the many. Whoever dreamed that one up did not know of the principle of the better idea. There's only one thing that goes through sixteen-inch armor plate and that's an idea. An idea progresses through a society in, you might say, logarithmic ratio[1] to the quality of the idea, i.e., its value in serving the needs of the times. Societies have been most remarkably and rapidly changed not through violence but through the introduction of a new idea. Violence merely stirs up all the old ideas and throws them into the air—then they all come back down again and we find the commissars[2] wearing different colored coats.

What about education? Is there a better idea?

In education we are dealing with any and all kinds of teaching or learning, nonacademic and academic. It is the science of getting data into analytical memory, of weighting[3] and comparing data, of computing and placing the computed solutions into action.

---

1   **logarithmic ratio**: A *logarithm*, most simply, is how many times you need to multiply a number, say 10, by itself to get a number, say 1000. In this case, the logarithm is 3, because you have to multiply 10 by itself 3 times to get 1000. A *logarithmic ratio* would be a ratio where one number changes very dramatically with small changes to the other number. Using the example just given of multiplying 10 by itself a certain number of times, the ratios would go 1 to 10, 2 to 100, 3 to 1000 and so on. As the first number increases by one, the second number increases by ten times.

2   **commissar**: a top government official in the Union of Soviet Socialist Republics in the first half of the 20th century.

3   **weight(ing)**: assign(ing) importance or value to something.

The primary rule guiding this is to forgo those things which do not keep reason reigning. If one wishes an individual to learn anything, academic or nonacademic, one must avoid any reduction of reasoning power, of full alertness on the part of the individual.

ALTITUDE INSTRUCTION

All teaching of an academic character has a tendency to be altitude[4] instruction, which is to say that the facts are handed from a higher plane of learning to the individual on a lower plane of learning. Instructors of the past have been all too prone to teach rather in the fashion that one feeds a boa constrictor—with a stuffing machine.

Children are fixated by parental threat of disapproval or punishment if they do not learn. They pass their early preschool years, often, in being "educated" into "social habits" from a level of high authority. They are given manifestoes rather than data. Most of their "social habits," which would have come naturally as they progressed, become something on the order of hypnotic suggestions. Indeed, the hypnotic suggestion is only an intensified form of altitude teaching; the reasoning power of the person is shut down, the operator then proceeds to pour in a lot of material which the subject, awake, accepts verbatim, literally—and, whatever the hypnotist of the past contended, harmfully.

FIXED DATA AND PUSH-BUTTON "REASONING"

There are very few things which can be used by the individual as unevaluated, fixed data. The multiplication table, spelling to some extent, and some other limited data, can be "learned" this way. But a datum such as "all cats are black" or "women are dangerous" as an unevaluated and fixed datum is a piece of insanity that will destroy the individual's reasoning on the subject of cats or women. For this individual, the word "cats" or "women" is a sort of *push button* that activates irrationality, or *push-button thought*. As such fixed data compound, the individual is less and less able to reason.

---

4 **altitude**: meaning from a position of superiority, higher status.

In the First World War, several nations were launched into an action which destroyed millions of their peoples by this push-button "reasoning." *Gott* (God) was with the Germans. And God was with everybody else. And the world had to be safe for Germany and democracy. A populace thoroughly "educated" in this country about the "devil" had only to be shown that the Kaiser[5] was the devil before it proceeded to attack the Kaiser. Whether the United States was right or wrong about going to war is beside the point, for the whole war was wrong, as wrong as this whole push-button "reasoning."

Such bits of fixed data are sown through the minds of people and through their cultures, rendering them prone to irrational stampedes. If an individual can be so thoroughly wrong, what of the child who lacks sufficient experience to steer a clear path through his or her small world?

Thus we must take into account this matter of teaching to individuals not fully reasoning and alert. Teach to an individual under heavy stress and what follows goes in rather like hypnotic suggestion. The person cannot reason on the data, but can only react. The struggle of humankind in the past has developed more and more into a struggle of push buttons against push buttons rather than reason against reason. Define "freedom" as something good to schoolchildren, then redefine it as state control when they are adults and they still cheer for freedom although they may have slave-chain galls an inch deep around their ankles and spend their time blessing the very chains that gall them.

Semantics[6] is a vital subject when one considers the push-button mechanism, for when one deals with fixed data, one is not dealing with reason, one is dealing with reaction.

Education, then, to be effective, no matter if it is the education a mother gives the infant or the professor gives the collegiate, must avoid becoming positive suggestion if it is to produce anything like an effective being.

---

5 **Kaiser**: reference to German Kaiser (emperor) Wilhelm II who was also king of Prussia at the time, instrumental in inciting tensions leading to World War I.

6 **semantics**: the study of words and their meanings.

A LIFETIME OF ALTITUDE INSTRUCTION

This sort of a situation may be found almost anywhere: Bill is a steam engineer; he knows quite a bit about steam engines and steam plants. One day his company shifts to diesel. Exit Bill. The excuse, perhaps, is that he is too old to learn something new and certainly he could not learn about diesels. Tracing one such case one finds at each step of Bill's life altitude teaching.

First, he had to mind his parents and older people and do what he was told.

Second, he had to learn what he was taught in school or get flunked and have the school fall in on him, or his parents send him into the cold world—or at least that was the impression given.

Third, we find he was educated into believing that a secure man had a specialized job.

Fourth, he was never given any change on that job so that he could become adaptable.

In the end, like the maker of buggy whips[7], he sees a careless world pass him by.

The errors here are standard. There is no slightest reason why a child must accept his or her parents literally and be punished with physical pain for not so accepting mandates, which are perhaps workable in childhood but are a terrible liability when the child becomes an adult.

On the second point, any school which teaches with threat and altitude by the examination and grade system is teaching by positive suggestion and has about as much appeal to reason as the penal code of Devils Island[8], and any instruction it gives forth is of minor value for reasons which will follow.

---

7 **buggy whip**: whip specifically designed for use on horses pulling horse-drawn carriages, which became obsolete with the introduction and eventual proliferation of the automobile.

8 **Devils Island**: a tiny offshore island of French Guiana (a region of France located in northeastern South America, just north of Brazil) which was the site of a penal colony for French political prisoners started in 1852. Prisoners received brutal and inhuman treatment, including being chained together and whipped. Devils Island became synonymous with brutal treatment. Its operations ceased in 1953.

The third point is an example of propaganda, always a thing of fixed data. A specialist has reduced his security by narrowing his gaze to one channel and reducing his adaptability. There is nothing wrong with being the world's greatest remover of the liver so long as one can also play the fiddle well enough to live or perform some other remunerative task, preferably less dependent upon the hands. Palsy[9] and accident may make one the person who was *once* the world's greatest remover of the liver, and that pays for no chow. Further, society says that a job is the thing, that a job is security, and that one is a good citizen when one has a regular job. Actually, that person, who to eat, depends upon another to furnish a job is very insecure. For oh, the ease with which the pink slip can turn up some Saturday and oh, the ease, in a totalitarianism, with which one can become *persona non grata* through disliking the strawberries the administration insists that all should eat. The only security is an ability to take care of oneself, family and friends no matter what economics turn up and that is a generality which is not answered by a job.

The fourth point is that a person's mind is alert only so long as it is learning.

This is not then the study of how to get A in a classroom of some authoritarian university, although it can include that too. It is the science of how to learn and how to teach in such a way as to preserve the alertness of the individual's mind and to make it possible for the individual to place into action a maximum of solutions based on a minimum of data.

PRECAUTIONS FOR THE STUDENT

As to learning, one should take precautions against having altitude teaching thrown at one in such a way as to form fixed data.

Just because Professor Blimp is one of the eight men in the country who has memorized the collected works of Sir Thomas Browne[10] is no reason why anyone should respect Professor Blimp.

---

9 **palsy**: a condition of uncontrolled shaking of the body or one or more of its parts.
10 **Sir Thomas Browne**: (1605-1682) An English scientist and author of varied works.

Just because Instructor Snoozer says one's prose style is bad is no reason to believe him. Snoozer couldn't sell a want ad to the *Whoosis Gazette*; he wouldn't be an instructor if he knew enough about prose to write it.

Just because Dean Sturgis can look stern is no reason to believe what he says about nuclear physics. It will all be old hat and utterly wrong by the time you graduate anyway. And if you are being flunked out, be consoled—the only independent characters who have created anything worthwhile in the past five centuries were all flunked out.

Further, one's parents do not die of grief if one gets a B. They may say so, but scientific investigations have established the fact that no parents have ever expired from this cause.

In learning, study what you want to know, think what you want to think about it, recognize educational institutionalism for the bogus straw man it is, and keep your mind whirring.

PRECAUTIONS FOR THE TEACHER

As to teaching, that is a more responsible and a more serious matter.

The first vital principle in teaching the person is to do everything possible to keep his reasoning power turned on and aligned with the subject on a rational plane. This instantly rules out rostrum pomposity and manifestoes, grades, examinations, mass teaching—all tricks of altitude whereby the data, forced in, becomes fixed, unevaluated data.

Shakespeare has to become a playwright, not a god, and if the student doesn't like him that's Shakespeare's fault. Calculus[11] has to become a bunch of tricks by which one accomplishes, by abstractions, certain useful results, not a tangle of dy/dx summate and excruciate[12] (and if the minus sign is wrong one flunks calculus not algebra where the student should have learned minus signs). Biology

---

11 **Calculus** is a type of mathematics used to measure motion, change and accumulation with wide-ranging applications, including in the fields of physics, computers, finance, engineering, architecture and aviation.

12 **"dy/dx summate and excruciate"** is a significant-sounding, humorous phrase that uses a few calculus terms.

becomes the study of life, not the study of somebody's book who will be as outmoded as Aristotle's pendulum.[13] Civics becomes the study of how one runs a country, not how one parrots a politician. History becomes the story of a lot of fellows who did things, not a string of dates attached to some improbable heroes who weren't that way at all. And chemistry becomes "that changing science with which you can do some very fine things if you carefully disbelieve our present theories." And philosophy becomes a study of how to be a philosopher, which is to think and synthesize, not a dull memorization of a lot of fellows who wrote a lot more than they knew about.

In order to understand what is necessary in instructing, no matter if one is instructing a baby of two or a man or woman of twenty-one, it is necessary to know that all forcefully impressed data (whether by a spanking or a threat of a low grade) does the following:

1. makes the data unavailable to an individual's rational thinking processes,

2. reduces the force and therefore the efficiency and ability of the student,

3. may cause him or her serious trouble later in life, and

4. because humans are very complex animals and furiously try to measure up to the proper level of self-determinism, produces effects which cannot be calculated in advance and which may include rebellion, apathy, illness or worse.

THE EXAMINATION SYSTEM

The examination system employed is not much different from a certain hypnotic technique. One induces a state of confusion in the student by raising his anxieties of what may happen if he does not "pass." One then "teaches" at a mind which is anxious and confused. That mind does not then think rationally, it does not *reason*; it merely records and makes a pattern. If the pattern is sufficiently strong to be regurgitated verbatim on an examination paper, the student is then given a good grade and passed.

---

13 **Aristotle's pendulum**: In his book *Physica*, Aristotle provided an explanation of natural motion, explained later with reference to a pendulum. His explanations gradually proved insufficient and therefore outmoded as science advanced.

A good grade is supposed to be synonymous with a bright mind. It is actually, under the present system, only a measure of ability to receive and recall data without caviling at conclusions drawn by the instructor and no measure of the student's ability to do anything with the knowledge if ever transplanted into another environment. As to a student's ability to recall information, we find a condition which is no measure whatever of either intelligence or ability but only demonstrates a student's ability to recall by rote what he has heard or seen and set it down. In technical subjects a certain computational ability is necessary, but schools demand computation by rote and actually for any method given there may be many others.

Just bluntly, the principle of altitude examination teaching is 180 degrees wrong.

Where we have altitude teaching, somebody is a great authority. They hold their position by being a "great authority."

They're probably teaching some subject that has become far more complex than it should be. And they have become defensive down through the years as a sort of protective coating that they put up. In their mind, the subject will always be a little bit better known by them than by any student, and there are things to know in this subject which they wouldn't really let anybody else in on.

This is altitude instruction.

Then, in order to get people to sit very alertly and pay attention to this individual and do exactly as instructed, there is the other trick: the examination.

There is an anxiety created around this examination because the student is indoctrinated in the belief that if you fail school, if you don't pass, the world will fall in, the sun will go completely out of its firmament, you will be left to starve and die in the streets and everybody will hate you.

Little kids can actually look at it like that. They grow up with this anxiety around grades. They come forward to a point where when somebody says "examination" to them, it's a threat to Mama, Papa, love, general survival and everything else.

It's a terrific whip. And it has the potential of keeping people in a state of confusion.

ADJUSTING TO THE ENVIRONMENT OF WORK

By training students for years beyond the moment when nature decrees they jump out of the nest, another factor is entered—that of impeding adjustment to the environment of work. The environment which one should occupy for life should be experienced as early as possible so that facts can begin to align with actuality. For facts unaligned with actuality are so much excess baggage and actually impede the ability of the student to work efficiently when he or she finally does have a field where theory becomes, all of a sudden, actuality.

ENVIRONMENT AND DATA WEIGHT

Environment is another grossly overlooked factor in contemporary education, since environment is the one thing which can give data a proper weight. Many a navigator can sail the devil out of a ship in a classroom and get lost trying to find the end of a pier!

Education which is done against a strictly academic background is stultifying[14] and most of its importance is lost because it has not exercised the person's mind in weighting and deriving. A classroom is no proper place to learn to run a steam locomotive. The proper method would be to throw a student, as yet wholly uninformed, aboard a Malley[15] and give them the throttle on a clear piece of track. Baffled and balked by all the bright brass, the student would be sufficiently challenged to buckle down and learn and would have a feel of what was being learned—or would decide to be a cabinetmaker after all, and a lot of training hours would have been saved for the student and some badgered instructor.

An individual can be given rudimentary instruction in reading, writing, history, literature, music, manners and mathematics. Anyone keeping a person in school, as just school, beyond this is wasting the person's adulthood. One should be experiencing the environment of one's chosen profession from the age of at least fifteen. One would ideally be educated after that in short spurts in school as one desires to know more and educated by professionals in one's own business.

---

14 **stultifying**: made foolish, worthless or useless; robbed of strength, vigor, liveliness, interest.

15 **Malley**: also Mallet, a steam locomotive invented by Swiss engineer Anatole Mallet (1837-1919).

BETTER, NOT MORE

Better education, not more education, is what is needed. Indeed, if people have to spend more years at being educated than they do, the graduates will have only one voyage out into the world—the journey to the old folks' home over the hill.

There is no such thing as being overeducated. There *is* such a thing as being badly educated. The length of time in school is no criteria of either one.

CONCLUSION

Sadly, the blunders which are made in contemporary academic education are many.

Most fundamentally, education needs to be disassociated from scholasticism[16]. There are men who have never seen the inside of a university who are superior to and worth more to society than those who carried away the highest honors. Herbert Spencer[17] spent three years at school in all his life. Spinoza[18] spent a very few years and then was expelled. Francis Bacon[19], the man who gave us all the fundamentals of what we call now the scientific method, went to school three years, revolted against Aristotle, and left the halls of learning in a huff.

Actually, as one walks down the halls of learning and looks at the busts of the great therein, one is struck by the number who were not formally educated but took the world for their texts and professors. With some research, an individual might conclude that the surest way to succeed in any profession is to study something else at school!

---

16 **scholasticism**: narrow-minded and often self-important insistence on traditional scholarly doctrines and methods; scholarly conservatism. This term comes from a system of philosophical and religious teaching in medieval European universities. Based on a system of logic developed by Aristotle and the writings of early Christian leaders, medieval scholasticism emphasized tradition and strict rules or beliefs.

17 **Herbert Spencer**: (1820-1903) English philosopher, scientist and sociologist with knowledge spanning a wide range of fields and well over a million copies of his written works sold in his lifetime.

18 **Baruch Spinoza**: (1632-1677) Dutch philosopher, who believed in and practiced tolerance and benevolence while challenging many accepted ideas of his time, particularly religious ones.

19 **Francis Bacon**: (1561-1626) English philosopher, scientist, statesman, author, father of the "scientific method."

There is excellent reason for this and most educational centers would richly profit by some soul-searching. All through these centers, individuals of spirit and wit have been telling one another that something was wrong and trying to improve what they could and escape as much as possible the stigma of scholasticism.

So there is no question of blame, but only a hope of progress.

3

Solutions

WILLINGNESS TO LEARN

The self-determinism of the individual must, above all things, be left as intact as possible. The student should not be asked to work or study because somebody else decrees it. The moment exterior force is applied, the student combats that force and is distracted from the principal purpose, in education, of learning.

If the individual is unwilling to follow a vital course of study, the error does not lie with the individual. A child or an adult is thirsty for knowledge. A person will drink knowledge at great gulps. The unwillingness stems from (a) a failure to observe the necessity or use of the course or (b) mental blocks against studying that thing or that course. The moment the necessity of the learning is realized the student will pour in wattage on the subject. In a very young child little can be done about the mental blocks, but much can be done in changing the method of address to the subject so that it does not cause a reaction; i.e., if a child will not "set the table" try "lay out the plates."

EXERCISING THE MIND—THE IMPORTANCE OF GOALS

All training must have first a goal. Unless the student understands the purpose thoroughly and the intended use of the information, the data is unaligned and therefore relatively useless. True, an individual reevaluates data when a new purpose is at hand and will align data after it was received. But the delivery of data without first giving the purpose fails because the recipient of the information, having no assigned use for it, is much less interested in it than he or she would be and so does not compute with it, only records it. Thus the process is one of memory, and the mind is not exercised into deriving new data from the information it receives.

The actual training of an individual is an automatic process so long as purpose and use precede information. The individual's mind is busied in weighting values and doing computations to derive new data and when it fails by one method of computation it will learn or discover another one to make up the lack.

As with muscles, from the youngest infancy to death, the mind must be active, and it is active so long as it has goals. An individual uses his or her mind to accomplish something in the desire to enjoy it and then contemplates the accomplishment for a breath of space and unless there is an immediate new goal, becomes dissatisfied. Happiness can be considered the act of accomplishing, over not unknowable obstacles, new goals. Happiness is not the goal. It is the act of reaching toward and progressing toward the goal. It lies, in the briefest instant, in contemplating the accomplished. It lies for a brief time in contemplating what is to be accomplished before beginning upon it, but the main body of it lies in the field of active endeavor.

Whether one is teaching someone to eat with a fork or training someone in calculus, the principles are the same. There must be a good reason, first, before the person will use the fork and the person must understand that reason. There must be an equally good reason and use for calculus *as calculus,* not a grade or degree, before the person can be expected to derive much from it.

TEACHING THE STUDENT TO THINK WITH AND USE THE INFORMATION

How, in education itself, would we go about relaying information? Here we've got a complete problem of communication from beginning to end. It is not possible to relay to people data which they are going to use on any other level than a parity of levels.

You want data to get to people in such a way that they can get at it again, and if necessary, reevaluate it. In other words, you don't want data that would be hung up on the order of "You've got to believe this, and this is the way it is and it is this way because it is this way, and you're never going to be able to change your mind about it being this way, and it's going to be this way from here on out."

If a person was being educated in the field of engineering, for instance, and was unable to reevaluate all of this information, then fifteen years from now this person would be lucky to hold on with these young whippersnappers coming in who have more data, newer data.

So our problem then is to teach people to derive from the information we're teaching them the future information they will need, to give them information in a state where it can be reevaluated at any time, and to keep uninhibited their individual purposes and interests with regard to that information so that they can think with and use it.

COMPARISON TO THE REAL WORLD

Which leads us to another factor: The education which a person is receiving must have been consistently compared, step by step, to the known world. You can't step into an abstract in education and never compare it to things which can be actually sensed, measured or experienced.

In other words, education would not best be conducted in a school where the real world was very far away indeed.

An engineering education would probably best be conducted by engineers in the process of engineering. If you want to teach a person to build bridges, it would be all very well that he or she has the basic fundamentals of those textbooks—they contain a lot of fine information. But let's also see him or her out there walking around with people who build bridges.

I one time encountered somebody teaching calculus in this abstract, purposeless fashion. It didn't say in the textbook what you used calculus for. The instructor didn't say what calculus was or what it was for, and I noticed that everybody in this class—it was my calculus class, by the way—was just studying away and they were differentiating[1] and they were integrating and, boy, they were having a fine time. I sat back and wasted about two weeks. I was trying to figure out what you did with calculus before I let myself open to a barrage of calculus.

---

1 **differentiating/integrating**: terms used in calculus, which measures motion, change (differentiating) and accumulation (integrating).

I asked the instructor two or three times and he looked embarrassed and looked away hurriedly. It suddenly came to me that he didn't know too well either. He was a mathematician but he had never been through engineering, so he didn't know how an engineer used calculus. I finally found a little book by a fellow named Thompson,[2] and it started out with an example of what you did with calculus. I looked this and other things over for a while and then was perfectly willing to get down and study calculus.

DEFINING THE PURPOSE OF THE SUBJECT

The defined purpose then becomes a very important factor in education: "What is this information going to do for me in my business of survival? What sector does it cover? How important is it?"

And the individual has a right to look it all over, and when done, be able to say, "That doesn't look important to me," and after that leave it alone. Because there is no reason to try to force pieces of information into heads that are not going to do anything with them. And if they don't know what it's for, they're not going to do anything with it.

TEACHING WITH PARITY

How *should* students be taught so they can absorb information and learn data for their own use?

They should be taught on a parity basis, where *parity* refers to two or more people or things being on an equal level. In other words, "this is between friends," something like that—between acquaintances, fellows, teammates, where the teacher is not some "great authority" to be worshiped or feared and does not talk down to students, but is essentially on an equal level with the student, where the student feels comfortable approaching the teacher, questioning the data, and so on.

---

2 **Thompson**: Silvanus Phillips Thompson (1851–1916), author of *Calculus Made Easy.*

SAFEGUARDING THE STUDENT'S RIGHT TO THINK

The one thing that must be completely safeguarded in the human being in the process of education is that he or she must be permitted to think.

People can be taught the basic fundamentals of any subject.

And they can be taught to derive further information they may need on the subject.

And they should also be taught that they have a right to use this information, to think about it, figure out new things about it and execute with relationship to it.

If those things are safeguarded, you could then and only then call the person well educated.

INTRODUCING THE IDEA OF AN EDUCATIONAL ETHIC[3]

So we get another point in education which is very important: In the process of education, those things which are not known exactly must be labeled as such. If it's an inexactly known subject, let's teach it as an inexactly known subject; i.e., let's tell the student we're teaching it as such.

That would be educational honesty and it is something which should be part of the educational ethic. And all of these points being stressed here as desirable would form, when amalgamated, an educational ethic. It could be considered astonishing how lacking our culture is in any agreed upon educational ethic along these lines.

After all, what is the responsibility of the teacher and the institution to the person who is being educated? The kingpin around an institution is the person who is being educated, not the person who is doing the educating.

---

3 **ethic**: framework, system or set of principles concerning right and wrong, especially as accepted by an individual or a particular group; code of conduct.

DON'T PENALIZE STUDENTS—HELP THEM

Reduction of altitude would include the idea that people don't feel they have to take data just because somebody said so. They take data if it makes *sense* to them when they compare it to the real world, if it makes their *thinking* clearer, if it makes things better for them.

But nothing should be forced off on the student—*nothing*.

Furthermore, if there are some misunderstandings, help students clear them up. Students should not be penalized for misunderstandings. In other words, don't give them trouble because they have the wrong answer—try to help them so they can get a right answer.

That's a big difference. That's a complete reversal on the examination system, isn't it?

SUMMARY

The story of the growth of knowledge is the story of individuals, not the story of societies. Individuals make societies, societies only modify and moderate or warp individuals. All education is the education of individuals, not the education of the masses.

Pertinent to this last, in the days since Jefferson the theory has grown largely held that philosophers and conquerors came into being as products of an age and a society, and if one had not occupied their boots another would have done so. An examination of history disproves utterly such a tenet. Humankind goes on from the milestone of one individual to the milestone of the next. Human history is the track along which men and women, here and there, have been strong or brilliant and have changed the complexion of the road.

This tenet has colored all modern education, which then found an excuse to assembly-line individuals, making them conform like so many dolls.

Actually this piece of error, raising up a false standard of groupism, has through the policies of education spoiled perhaps thousands of individuals who would have been of considerable worth to the society. The paintings, plays, compositions of music, cathedrals and states which might have been, had not bad education stepped in the way, are a real and not imaginary loss to humankind.

Aristotle was a great man, but scholasticism has bled our minds and drained our energies through the collapse of the Roman Empire, through the Dark Ages, through the American university and to the H-bomb.

An educational system which slaughters genuine capability has a wide effect. Social leveling to the arithmetic mean and to the mediocre sets up the sheep society as the model, and sheep can be stampeded because they are easily frightened and are not particularly rational. Only highly rational individuals who are the product of excellent individual educations can stay a stampede.

An educational program which begins with the child's parents, progresses through kindergarten and grade school, through high school and into college and preserves at every step the individuality, the native ambitions, intelligence, abilities and dynamics[4] of the individual, is the best bastion against not only mediocrity but any and all enemies of humankind.

---

4   See chapter 10, section "The Eight Dynamics."

4

Educational Axioms

(1950)

DATA EVALUATION

Here are a few axioms that mainly concern the weighting[1] of data, problems, solutions and conclusions. The most serious hole in all contemporary education is its failure to recognize the importance of data weight. The instructor cannot weight data for the pupil. The pupil must have a sufficient goal so as to weight the data him- or herself.

- In education, a datum is as important as it contributes to the solution of problems.

- Problems and solutions are as important as they are related to survival.

- A datum is valid only when it can be sensed, measured or experienced.

- A foremost part of all education is the evaluating of the importance of data.

- A datum is important only in relationship to other data.

- A datum is as valuable as it has been evaluated.

AUTHORITARIANISM: ARBITRARY VS. NATURAL LAW

Further pertinent axioms follow:

- Arbitrary law is anything formulated and promulgated by reason of man's will, to be enforced by threat or punishment or merely disapprobation.

---

1 **weight(ing)**: assign(ing) importance or value to something.

- Natural law is enforced by nature. Logic adapts decision and conduct to nature or adapts nature.

- The amount of arbitrary law existing in a society is a direct index to the inability of that society to be rational and to the irrationality of the members of that society.

- Only in the face of irrationality is force necessary.

All things or entities which are irrational are handled by force in ratio to their irrationality. For example, inanimate matter and free energy, possessing no rationality, are handled only by force.

Life forms, on the other hand, are handled with force less and less as they ascend up the scale from irrationality to rationality. A fully logical entity not only should not be handled by force, but excepting only cataclysms, cannot be handled by force.

Any subject should be called and treated as an art until its natural laws, or some of them, are known. The formulation of rules before the natural laws are known introduces arbitrary factors which inhibit action and destroy reason. As much flexibility and variability must be employed in any educational subject as the subject contains, which is to say that so long as the natural laws are unknown, the subject must be taught with the fullest possible awareness that they are unknown and the fact that they are unknown must be a part of the teaching.

Authoritarianism could be defined as *the introduction of arbitrary law where no natural law is known, yet maintaining that the arbitrary law is the natural law*.

GOALS AND PRINCIPLES OF EDUCATION

These further axioms follow:

- It is a prime purpose of education to increase the self-determinism of the individual.

- It is a goal of education to sort the arbitrary from the natural.

- It is a principle of education to properly label that which is arbitrary and that which is natural.

- It is directly opposed to the best interests of education and a society to give force to any opinion of whatever kind and to force that opinion upon any student or individual.

- The maintenance of a high level of self-determinism is more important in educating than the maintenance of order.

As the irrationality of an individual forces itself against others, so must force be applied against the individual, but in such a way as to decrease the exhibition of the irrationality and with due regard to the health and self-determinism of the individual.

CONCLUSION

In this context, we could provide the following definition of education:

The science which formulates reasonability and conduct in the face of natural laws and advances techniques to inculcate natural principles and laws into the mind. Its goal is maximal training in minimal time in the activity of living, preserving maximal freedom of use of the lessons gained.

Education must raise the level of rationality and increase and reinforce the basic purpose of the individual if it is to result in a betterment of the individual or of society.

Specifically, what one wants in education is to teach a person how to absorb, use and evolve knowledge. On that basis alone, one could remove from the educational system all the gimmicks and gimcracks[2] that have been added in and have done something very worthwhile.

---

2 **gimcrack**: a showy or expensive object or gadget that has little or no real value or use.

5

More Fundamentals on Knowledge and Learning

(1950)

THE VALUE OF KNOWLEDGE

A person takes various routes toward understanding and one should never despise any of these.

You might say the greatest enemies of the human race have been those individuals who have destroyed knowledge or who have destroyed bodies of knowledge.

Julius Caesar, quite in addition to ordering the right hands cut off of fifty thousand human beings, put a torch to the library at Alexandria and destroyed, in that moment, the only existing storehouse of knowledge of several civilizations! What was in the library at Alexandria (which I believe, by the way, was destroyed five times in all) we now can't say. We can hardly guess. Knowledge was there which comes to us now only on a byroute.

And yet humanity has come forward along its track and has brought forward knowledge. We are a great civilization today because we can communicate knowledge readily and rapidly through the printed word and other means. Actually, a civilization progresses somewhat in ratio to its ability to communicate.

Knowledge, then, is the very stuff of which survival is made and should therefore be understood for what it is.

AXIOMS ON KNOWLEDGE

We could add a couple axioms concerning knowledge. Here's one:

- Every datum is as valuable as it explains other data.

Let's take as an example a basic mathematical equation—the Pythagorean theorem. This simple theorem explains an awful lot about surveying, to say the least. So we say the Pythagorean theorem is a very valuable datum. It is as valuable as it explains other data.

Another axiom:

- A datum can only be evaluated in terms of data of comparable magnitude.

In other words, don't try to evaluate a mountain by comparing it to a grain of sand. One evaluates mountains in terms of mountains—same order of magnitude.

This is the difficulty that people get into when trying to communicate with people in an undeveloped country. I was once trying to teach a class of little Chamorro[1] boys and girls—about the third grade I think they were—and they were supposed to be in the process of being taught English. Having joined my father on the U.S. Naval Base in Guam, I was about sixteen years old in territory that had been fairly chewed up in the process of the previous war. These little kids were ordered by the government to wear one article of clothing and they wore only shirts. And these shirts came down just above the navel. Some of them got real flashy when they were rich and wore only shoes!

These little kids were pretty cute. I tried to teach them English and a little bit about arithmetic, hygiene and the rest of the world. And on the first few of those topics, I could get along fine. But as soon as I struck that last topic, that was tough, because I tried to relate every datum I gave them to data which they had to hand. And naturally, they didn't have to hand data of comparable magnitude to the rest of the world.

---

1 **Chamorro**: people indigenous to the Mariana Islands, which include the island of Guam.

It recalls to mind when I was little and was reading about 1914, 1915, the Germans had done such-and-such and the French were retreating and the bombs were exploding and so on—and I was trying to understand this. I knew at that time one valley. It was a big valley. It was about fifty miles in diameter. I actually knew more world than most kids did at that time because I could look about seventy-five miles through the clear mountain air of Montana and I could see the Bitterroot Range[2]. Well, that was a pretty big world. But I was absolutely convinced that just beyond the Bitterroot Range raged the whole war! That was the rest of the world. All I had to compare it with was the valley. And naturally, if I compared the rest of the world with the valley, then the rest of the world must be just about the size of the valley!

Trying to relay information to these kids was similar. I tried to tell them about a skyscraper. One little kid figured on this, and he figured and he figured. I think the biggest skyscraper we had at the time was the Woolworth Building[3]—I was trying to tell him about the Woolworth Building and he figured on it for a long time.

I came in one morning early and I thought he had forgotten about this problem long since, but there he stood on a stool at the blackboard and he was drawing nipa huts[4] to the height necessary to make the seventy-three, seventy-four stories—or whatever it was—of the Woolworth Building. He was building them all with stilts. These were the buildings he had seen—this was the building we were in, right there. And he got up there to about twenty-five nipa huts and finally decided that these confounded nipa huts piled up this way were going to fall over. So, obviously, the thing could not be done and I was a liar! He had no datum of comparable magnitude.

A datum is only as understandable as it compares or is compared to data of comparable magnitude.

---

2 **Bitterroot Range**: a portion of the Rocky Mountains located in eastern Idaho and western Montana.

3 **Woolworth Building**: a sixty-story skyscraper built in New York City in 1913, known for nearly twenty years as the world's tallest office building.

4 **nipa hut**: a type of stilt house common to the Philippines and other South Pacific locations, named for the nipa palm tree's long feathery leaves often used for the roofs.

MIMICRY

Mimicry is number one on the learning agenda. A human's ability to mimic teaches the person more than any other single factor. You ask a man how to fire an arrow out of a bow and with no bow or arrows to hand he starts explaining how this is done. "Well, you take the arrow in your right hand and you take the bow in your left hand and you present it before you in a horizontal position and then you plant your feet one slightly advanced of the other and the right foot at a forty-five degree angle from the left foot at a distance of eighteen inches...." Clearly, this doesn't work.

On the other hand, on a mimicry basis with bows and arrows to hand he says, "Well, that's very simple, you just hold the bow right here, yes, just like that. Then place the arrow right here...yes, that's right. Now, watch how I do this...." Providing a good model to mimic and letting the person watch for a little while and then go over it with the bow and arrow in hand, this is the normal way of learning most things. If they're a bad mimic, they'll have a hard time. But if they are a good mimic and they're not otherwise impeded, they will not only be able to hold the bow properly but they'll be able to hit the mark, just like that.

Children will mimic anything. Understanding this, people should of course take time out to give the child something to mimic. You'll find the education of the child just increasing by leaps and bounds if you do this, because the child's only frame of reference is to mimic. The child wants to be a grown-up and he or she is going to try to act like grown-ups act. Well, you should be sure to give the child a grown-up to act like.

STARTING WITH THE PURPOSE OF A SUBJECT

The first thing stated in any subject should be its purpose. For example, "This is the subject of dancing. People study it because most people enjoy dancing and seeing other people dance. It's fun to dance to music and there's lots of kinds of dances you can learn and it's good exercise." Or some such.

All subjects should start out with a stated purpose. And this purpose should be very carefully delineated against the real world of the person who is doing the studying. In other words, what we're trying to teach couldn't be taught thoroughly unless the student could evaluate it against his or her own real world.

TAKING INTO ACCOUNT THE REAL WORLD OF THE STUDENT

So the first study done by any teacher should be this: What is the real world of the person we are teaching? And I'm afraid few professors or teachers know this; they have not made a good, thorough study of the real world of their student. They've had some idea on the subject but once they studied it they then tended to say, in the case of young children, "It's delusion."

Well, it may be delusion to the teacher who doesn't see the child's real world. The teacher, however, has to take solidly into account that real world of a child if he or she wants to teach the child. And the teacher actually has to accept this as a real world if they expect this child to learn a thing.

For instance, I had to accept the real world of these Chamorro children before I could teach them anything. When I evaluated everything from that perspective, the problem resolved. I helped these kids understand a bit about trains, for example, by just building it up out of oxcart wheels and the like.

Educationally, you have to know what you're looking at. When you look at children and see them slugging away, you can often find that people have failed to evaluate the real world of a child. You certainly can't enter any information into a child that he or she can use unless you know the real world you are working with there.

Realize that this real world includes the possibility that at one fell swoop one can become Roy Rogers,[5] Hopalong Cassidy,[6] Captain Starbuck[7] or Captain Midnight[8]. That one can take an old apple box and have there a roaring fire, a beautiful dinner all ready to serve—a perfectly edible dinner which can be tasted! Then there are their emotional values, which are also very important. And when one fails to look it over and appreciate what those emotional values are, one isn't likely to communicate with them very well.

---

5 **Roy Rogers**: (1911–1998) American cowboy star of movies and television from the late 1930s to the 1950s.

6 **Hopalong Cassidy**: a fictional cowboy hero of radio, television and film in the 1930s and 1940s.

7 **Captain Starbuck**: this appears to be a made-up name for a fictional hero.

8 **Captain Midnight**: the name given an American comic strip and radio character from the 1940s.

CONFINING A CHILD

Understanding the real world of a child might include the realization that the last place in the world you'd want to put the child for instruction would be in a closed room.

Run a little experiment of having a child sit on your lap and just put your arms around the child loosely. The child will sit there, contented. Then just lock your hands around his or her tummy. Instantly the child will squirm and fight to get away from you. Life is not to be trapped by space or limited in position in time. It's simply not to be. And children are very much alive.

So you put a child in a room under confinement, under restraint and you expect the child to learn anything? It's no wonder so many children get to be fifteen years of age and can't even write intelligibly.

EXCESSIVELY LEADING A CHILD

There's another factor that you must not avoid in looking this over and that is that the path of learning must not be particularly smooth. Individuals are so composed as to overcome obstacles toward known goals and are not aided at all if you do all of the leading. You can't lead them, you can't drive them: the business of leading or driving is native in the child and if you keep your hands off it the child will continue along the line. Anytime anyone tries to lead or drive the child excessively, the ability within the child to surge toward goals is interrupted.

SELF-DETERMINISM AND EFFICIENCY

An individual is not a machine being driven along rails or in grooves. Individuals are either "self-determining" their courses in existence to some degree or they're not. And if they are "self-determining" their courses in existence, believe me, they will do it efficiently. If they're not, believe me, they won't do it efficiently, no matter how many whips are laid upon their backs.

OVERSELLING THE CHILD ON LEARNING

When one tries very much and very hard to encourage a child as to the value of some study, tries to oversell the child an idea, you will see that it's quite destructive—the child is liable to get there and find out it wasn't that good. The only thing you can do is tell the child the truth as near as you know it and fit it into the framework of his or her own understanding.

This applies to the university student as well as the kindergarten child. It's the same thing. You tell them as near as you know, by their own frame of reference, what it is they are going toward as far as you have investigated the subject and you leave it strictly up to them whether or not they are going to go there.

When children start getting into formal education, one still has to understand their frame of reference, giving them a good and adequate purpose, showing them what lies ahead—not leading or driving them toward it. If done well, you will have at the end of that run all the way through university a thoroughly educated person—a *real* educated person.

CONCLUSION

I'm afraid the difference in education which people can get is very wide. I am also afraid that in this year of 1950, the education which is given in grade school, high school and the university is rather thoroughly destructive toward the initiative and abilities of human beings.

In the U.S., we graduated 280,000 Bachelors of Art year before last—280,000 people is a lot of people. And the effect upon the society is going to be, well, it's better than nothing. These people are going to get in there and pitch, most of them, on what native and acquired skills they have. But supposing instead we had graduated 280,000 accomplished artists in their own field. This society, within the generation, would have changed its whole face and complexion to something far better than we have now.

A valid end and goal of any society, as it addresses the problem of education, would be to raise the ability, the initiative and the cultural level, and with all these the survival level of that society. When a society forgets any one of these things, it is destroying itself by its own educational mediums.

6

Causation
and Knowledge

(1956)

KNOWLEDGE—CAUSE AND EFFECT

The greatest philosophical clamor or quarrel has been waged around the subject of "knowledge" and there is nothing preposterous on the subject of knowledge that cannot be found in one or another philosophical text.

For the purposes of this discussion, by knowledge we mean assured belief, that which is known, information, instruction, enlightenment, learning, practical skill. We mean data, factors and whatever can be thought about or perceived.

The reason why knowledge has been misunderstood is because what is normally thought of as knowledge is only half the answer. By definition, knowledge has been thought of as that which is perceived or learned or taken from another source. This patently means that when one learns, one is being an effect.

Opposed to this we have the neglected half of existence, which is the *creation* of knowledge, the creation of data, the creation of thought, the causative consideration, self-evolved ideas as opposed to ideas otherwise evolved.

There is *cause* and *effect*. Cause could be defined as emanation. It could be defined also, for purposes of communication, as source-point. If you consider a river flowing to the sea, the place where it began would be the source-point or cause and the place where it went into the sea would be the effect-point, and the sea would be the effect of the river. The person firing the gun is cause; the person receiving the bullet is effect. The one making a statement is causing a communication; the one receiving the statement is the effect of the communication. A basic definition of communication is cause-distance-effect.

It might be observed that almost all anxieties and upsets in human relations come about through an imbalance of cause and effect. The entire subject of responsibility is a study of cause and effect in that a person who wants no responsibility is anxious to be an effect only and a person who can assume responsibility must also be willing to be causative.

CREATE AND RECEIVE

One must be willing at once to create new data, statements, assumptions, considerations and to receive ideas, assumptions, considerations.

Study, investigation, receiving education and similar activity are all effect activities and result in the assumption of less responsibility. If a person feels they must gather all of their data from elsewhere, they are then the effect of knowledge and they tend to reduce their own ability to form, make or create knowledge.

The way to paralyze a nation entirely and to make it completely ungovernable would be to forbid education of any kind within its borders and to inculcate into every person within it the feeling that they must not receive any information from anybody about anything.

To make a nation governable it is necessary to hold a kindly view of education and to honor educative persons and measures.

To conquer a land it is not necessarily efficient to overwhelm them with guns. Educative measures are then necessary in order to bring about some sort of agreement amongst the people themselves as well as between the conqueror and the subdued. Only in this way could one have a smoothly running society or civilization.

In other words, two extremes could be reached, neither one of which is desirable by the individual. The first extreme could be reached by emphasis only upon self-created data or information. This would bring about not only a lack of interpersonal relations, but also an anxiety to have an effect on others which would, as it does in barbaric peoples, result in social cruelty unimaginable in a civilized nation.

The other extreme would be to forbid in its entirety any self-created information and to condone only data or ideas generated by others than self. Here we would create an individual with no responsibility, so easily handled that they would be only a puppet.

Self-created data is then not a bad thing, neither is received data, but one without the other to hold it in some balance will result in something undesirable.

Historically, there have been cultures where the way of life included a contempt for the ideas of others and an emphasis on brutality and savagery. At the other extreme, there have been cultures slavishly dedicated to ancient scholars but incapable of generating sufficient leadership abilities in their own people to continue, without bloodshed, a nation.

We have noted the individual who must be the only one who can make a decision or take command, whose authority is dearer than the comfort or state of millions (Napoleon[1], Hitler, Kaiser Wilhelm, Frederick of Prussia, Genghis Khan, Attila). We have known, too, scholars who have studied themselves into blindness and are the world's greatest authority on government or some such thing, who yet cannot themselves manage their bank accounts or a dog with any certainty.

Here we have, in either case, a total imbalance. The world-shakers are themselves unwilling to be an effect of any kind (and all the men just named were arrant personal cowards) and we have the opposite, a person who would not know what you were talking about if you told them to get an idea of their own.

---

1   **Napoleon Bonaparte** (1769-1821) was a French military and political leader who conquered much of Europe in the early 19th century but at great cost, losing half a million of his own soldiers in one famously unsuccessful Russian campaign. *Adolph Hitler* (1889-1945) was a German politician, leader of the Nazi party, dictator, initiator of World War II and the murder of over six million innocent Jewish people. *Kaiser Wilhelm* (1859-1941) was the bombastic German emperor instrumental in inciting tensions leading to World War I. *Frederick of Prussia* (also known as Fredrick II or Frederick the Great) (1712-1786) was King of Prussia and immediately upon taking the throne launched an eight-year war against Austria to be followed several years later by another seven years of war during which his own army suffered tremendous losses. *Genghis Kahn* (1162-1227), as first in a line of Mongol rulers, conquered most of Eurasia, often through ruthless massacre of civilian populations. *Atilla the Hun* (circa 406-453) led armies that terrorized much of the Roman Empire, burning down whole towns and indiscriminately slaughtering civilians on the way to building a vast empire in less than ten years.

We see another example of this in the fundamental laws of warfare. A body of troops, to be effective, must be able to attack and to defend. Its implements must be divided 50% for attack and 50% for defense. In other words, even in a crude activity such as warfare, we find that no successful outcome is possible unless the troops can devote half of their energies to attack and half of them to defense.

The person who would give must be willing to receive. The person who would receive must be willing to give. When this is not the case, problems result.

KNOW AND NOT-KNOW

Whether one is creating or receiving information, one must retain one's ability to know. Less often recognized, yet of equal importance, is retaining one's ability to not-know.

All thought consists of knowing, not knowing, and the shades of gray between.

Education itself can only become burdensome when one is unable to not-know it.

The abilities of knowing and "not-knowing" can be understood in regard to time. Remembering is the process of knowing the past. Forgetting is the process of not-knowing the past. Prediction, knowing the future. Living "only for today," not-knowing the future.

CONCLUSION

It is necessary that one be able to create, to receive, to know and to not-know information, data and thoughts. Lacking any one of these skills, for they are skills, no matter how native they may be to an individual, one is apt to get into a chaos of thinking or learning.

You can, in fact, look at any eccentric or irrational person and discover rapidly, by an inspection of them, which one of these four factors they are violating. They are either unable to know or not-know their own created thoughts, or they are unable to know or not-know the thoughts of others.

An education which addresses equally each of these abilities in relation to knowledge, improving all and neglecting none, will improve the ability of the individual and his or her general capability in living.

7

Teaching: An Educational Ethic

(1951)

Regrettably, what passes for *education* today is practically without ethics. More often than not, it looks something like this:

Students are permitted to come in and study. They are tolerated while there. They are given the information, they are examined to see if they know the information, and then when everybody is sure their heads now contain some of this information, they dust their hands and crow proudly over their great task done.

That's not the way to do it. It can be done better.

The adoption, promulgation and practice of a true educational ethic would probably raise the general alertness of a whole nation within a couple of generations, to a point nobody ever dreamed of before.

Toward that end, here are ten points on teaching intended to fill the need for an educational ethic.

~

If one wishes a subject to be taught with maximal effectiveness, one should:

1. Present it in its most interesting form.

    a. Demonstrate its general use in life.

    b. Demonstrate its specific use to the student in life.

2. Present it in its simplest form (but not necessarily its most elementary).

   a. Gauge its terms to the understanding of the student.

   b. Use terms of greater complexity only as understanding progresses.

3. Teach it with minimal altitude (prestige).

   a. Do not assume importance merely because of a knowledge of the subject.

   b. Do not diminish the stature of students or their own prestige because they do not know the subject.

   c. Stress that importance resides only in individual skill in *using* the subject and, as to the instructor, assume prestige only by the *ability* to use it and by no artificial caste system.

4. Present each step of the subject in its most fundamental form with minimal material derived therefrom by the instructor.

   a. Insist only upon definite knowledge of axioms and theories.

   b. Coax into action the student's mind to *derive* and *establish* all data which can be derived or established from the axioms or theories.

   c. *Apply* the derivations as *action* insofar as the class facilities permit, coordinating data with reality.

5. Stress the values of data.

   a. Inculcate the individual necessity to evaluate axioms and theories in relative importance to each other and to question the validity of every axiom or theory.

   b. Stress the necessity of individual evaluation of every datum in its relationship to other data.

6. Form patterns of computation in the individual with regard only to their usefulness.

7. Teach *where* data can be found or *how* it can be derived, not the recording of data.

8. Be prepared, as an instructor, to learn from the students.

9. Treat subjects as variables of expanding use which may be altered at individual will. Teach the stability of knowledge as resident only in the student's ability to apply knowledge or alter what he or she knows for new application.

10. Stress the right of individuals to select only what they desire to know, to use any knowledge as they wish, that they themselves own what they have learned.

PART TWO
Basic Principles

8

Integrity

PERSONAL INTEGRITY

WHAT IS TRUE FOR YOU is what you have observed yourself
And when you lose that you have lost everything.

What is personal integrity?
Personal integrity is knowing what you know—
What you know is what you know—
And to have the courage to know and say what you have observed.
And that is integrity
And there is no other integrity.

Of course we can talk about honor, truth, all these things,
These esoteric terms.
But I think they'd all be covered very well
If what we really observed was what we observed,
That we took care to observe what we were observing,
That we always observed to observe.

And not necessarily maintaining a skeptical attitude,
A critical attitude, or an open mind.
But certainly maintaining sufficient personal integrity
And sufficient personal belief and confidence in self
And courage that we can observe what we observe
And say what we have observed.

Nothing is true for you
Unless you have observed it
And it is true according to your observation.

That is all.

STUDYING WITH INTEGRITY

The only advice I can give you is to study a subject for itself and use it exactly as stated, then form your own opinions.

Study it with the purpose in mind of arriving at your own conclusions as to whether the tenets you have assimilated are correct and workable.

Do not allow the authority of any one person or school of thought to create a foregone conclusion within your sphere of knowledge.

Only with these principles of education in mind can you become a truly educated individual.

9 ARC Triangle

INTRODUCTION

The ability to understand and be understood is an important skill for a teacher.

There are three interrelated factors essential to achieving understanding. These three factors are affinity, reality, and the most important, communication.

AFFINITY

The word "affinity" refers here to a variable quality, a degree of attraction, love, liking or any other emotional attitude. It includes the idea of distance where complete affinity would be the ability to occupy the same space as something else.

Note that under affinity we have the various emotional responses, ranging from the highest to the lowest, and these are in part: enthusiasm, cheerfulness, conservatism, contented, boredom, antagonism, anger, fear, grief, apathy.

One can recognize in this scale of emotional tones (levels) the variable quality of affinity (attraction, love, liking or the lack thereof)—of which an entire study could be made, but is not here.

A brief study could be made, however, by observing a child—let's say a young girl— trying to acquire something. At first she is happy. She simply wants it. If refused, she then explains why she wants it. If she fails to get it and did not want it badly, she becomes bored and goes away. But if she wants it badly, she will get antagonistic about it. Then she will become angry. Then, that failing, she may lie about why she wants it. That failing, she goes into grief. And if she is still refused, she finally sinks into apathy and says she doesn't want it. Happily, one will also find this same scale of emotions playing out in reverse when a person low on the scale rises up to enthusiasm. (A graphic of this scale of emotions is given in Chapter 22 Scales.)

A child is full of affinity. Not only do children have affinity for father, mother, brothers, sisters and playmates but for their dogs, cats and stray dogs that happen to come around.

But affinity goes even beyond this. One can have a feeling of affinity for objects. There is a feeling of oneness with the earth, blue skies, rain, millponds, cartwheels and bullfrogs which is affinity.

It could also be noted here that affinity tends to bring about affinity. A person who is filled with the quality will automatically find people anywhere near them also beginning to be filled with affinity. It is a calming, warming, heartening influence on all who are capable of receiving and giving it.

REALITY

Another factor that contributes to understanding is reality.

Reality could be defined as "that which appears to be."

Reality is sensed through various channels. We see something with our eyes, we hear something with our ears, we smell something with our nose, we touch something with our hands, and we decide, then, that there is something there. We are in contact through our sense channels with it.

That with which we agree tends to be more real than that with which we do not agree. There is a definite coordination between agreement and reality. Those things are real which we agree are real. Those things are not real which we agree are not real. On those things upon which we disagree we have very little reality. An experiment based on this would be an even joking discussion between two people of a third person who is present. The two people agree on something with which the third person cannot agree. The third person will actually become less real to those two people.

Reality is fundamentally agreement. What we agree to be real is real.

COMMUNICATION

A third factor that contributes to understanding is communication.

There are many, many ways to communicate besides just talking. Two people can look at each other and be in communication. You can use the sense of touch. For example, you pet a cat and the cat all of a sudden starts to purr—you are in communication with the cat. Or you reach out and shake someone's hand and you are in communication with them.

You can probably think of many more ways communication can occur.

Simple "talking" and "writing" randomly, however, would not necessarily be communication. Communication is essentially something which is sent and which is received. The intention to send and the intention to receive must both be present in some degree before an actual communication can take place. Therefore one could have conditions which appeared to be communications which were not.

THE INTERRELATIONSHIP

These three points, affinity, reality and communication, can be thought of as forming a triangle. Unless you have two corners of a triangle, there cannot be a third corner. Desiring any corner of the triangle, one must include the other two.

Every one of the three points—affinity, reality and communication—is dependent on the other two, and every two are dependent on one. It is only necessary to improve one corner of this triangle in order to improve the remaining two corners. It is only necessary to improve two corners of the triangle to improve the third. You can't affect one point without affecting the other two, positively or negatively.

For example, it is very difficult to suffer a reversal of affinity without also suffering a blockage of communication and a consequent deterioration of reality.

Consider a lovers' quarrel: One of the pair offers affinity in a certain way to the other. This affinity is either reversed or not acknowledged. The first lover feels insulted and begins to break off communication. The second lover, not understanding this break-off, also feels insulted and makes the break in communication even wider. The area of agreement between the two inevitably diminishes and the reality of their relationship begins to go down. Since they no longer agree on reality, there is less possibility of affinity between them, and the situation continues to worsen.

Fortunately it works both ways. Anything which will raise the level of affinity will also increase the ability to communicate and add to the perception of reality. Falling in love is a good example of the raising of the ability to communicate and of a heightened sense of reality occasioned by a sudden increase in affinity. If it has happened to you, you will remember the wonderful smell of the air, the feeling of affection for the good solid ground, the way in which the stars seemed to shine brighter and the sudden new ability in expressing yourself.

Given these principles of affinity, reality and communication, how do you talk to a person?

You cannot effectively talk to a person if you have no interest in him or her. You would have to have some degree of affinity to discuss things with anyone. Your ability to talk to a person has to do with your emotional response to that person. Additionally, a communication to be received must approximate the affinity level of the person to whom it is directed.

For instance, an enthusiastic communication directed at a deeply saddened person would not get a good response, whereas a sad or sympathetic communication would.

The way to talk to a person, then, would be to find something to like about the person and to discuss something with which he or she can agree. If you do not have the first two conditions, it is fairly certain that the third condition will not be present, which is to say, without affinity and reality, you will not be able to communicate easily.

The affinity-reality-communication triangle is not an equilateral triangle. Affinity and reality are very much less important than communication. It might be said that the triangle begins with communication, which brings into existence affinity and reality.

UNDERSTANDING

One can then see how to achieve understanding. Understanding consists of affinity, reality and communication. When an individual's understanding is great, their affinity, reality and communication are quite high. When we have raised these three points, we have raised somebody's understanding.

The applications of these principles to teaching, learning and education are endless.

A-R-C

A word, ARC (pronounced by stating its letters, A-R-C), can be made from the initial letters of Affinity, Reality and Communication.

Used formally, it refers to the interrelationship of these three factors. Used informally it has come to mean simply good feeling, love or friendliness. For example: *Karen has a lot of ARC for horses. There has always been good ARC between us. The elderly woman had a personal policy of maintaining high ARC with the teenagers in her neighborhood.*

10 Dynamics and the Individual

INDIVIDUALITY AND INTELLIGENCE

There are just as many degrees and kinds of intelligence as there are children.

THE EIGHT DYNAMICS

There could be said to be a surge of energy within each of us, an urge or thrust toward survival. A motivating or energizing force, this impulse acts like a basic command: "Survive!"

From the Greek word *dunamikos,* from *dunamis* meaning "power; strength," this could be called the survival "dynamic."

For the purposes of understanding and assisting an individual, if we take a look at this survival dynamic through a magnifying glass, we find that in this one thrust there could be described eight divisions or compartments—eight survival "dynamics." These would be eight motives, motivations or urges in the direction of survival for that individual:

(1) self

(2) sex and family unit

(3) groups

(4) humankind

(5) living things (plants and animals)

(6) the physical universe

(7) spirits

(8) infinity or the Supreme Being[1]

---

1 Any belief in a spiritual existence and any belief in the concept of a Supreme Being are, of course, assumed by the editors to be personal in nature. This concept and discussion of the eight dynamics is forwarded with the intention of being inclusive to all, regardless of their beliefs or attitudes about matters of a spiritual or religious nature.

Each of these eight dynamics, these eight basic compartments of life, would represent an energetic urge in a certain direction, the urge to survive along a certain course. They could best be represented as a series of concentric circles wherein the first dynamic would be the center and each new dynamic would be successively a circle outside it.

Let's look at each of these dynamics a bit more closely.

The *first dynamic* is the urge toward existence as one's self. Here we have individuality expressed fully.

The *second dynamic* is the urge toward existence as a sexual activity. This dynamic actually has two divisions. Second dynamic (a) is the sexual act itself. Second dynamic (b) is the family unit, including the rearing of children.

The *third dynamic* is the urge toward existence as groups of individuals. Any group, or part of an entire class, could be considered to be part of the third dynamic. The school, the society, the town, the nation are each *part* of the third dynamic and each one *is* a third dynamic.

The *fourth dynamic* is the urge toward existence as or of humankind. Whereas one race would be considered a third dynamic, all the races would be considered the fourth dynamic.

The *fifth dynamic* is the urge toward existence of the animal kingdom. This includes all living things, whether vegetable or animal, the fish in the sea, the beasts of the field or of the forest, grass, trees, flowers or anything directly and intimately motivated by life.

The *sixth dynamic* is the urge toward existence as the physical universe, which is composed of matter, energy, space and time.

The *seventh dynamic* is the urge toward existence as or of spirits. Anything spiritual, with or without identity, would come under the heading of the seventh dynamic.

The *eighth dynamic* is the urge toward existence as infinity. This could also be identified as the Supreme Being.

INDIVIDUALITY AND THE DYNAMICS

Though none of these dynamics is considered more important than any other one of them in terms of orienting an individual, it will be found among individuals that each person stresses one of the dynamics more than the others, or may stress a combination of dynamics as more important than other combinations.

While the dynamics are not of equal importance, one to the next, the ability of an individual to thrive on each dynamic could be considered an index of that individual's ability to live most fully.

A CAUTIONARY NOTE

The act of putting something into a child's memory and then seeing if the child can recall it later is no test of education.

A child not able to easily recall things may be much more intelligent and may have a much stronger survival dynamic than a child with excellent recall ability and low dynamic.

The child with the high dynamic, further, will rebel against authoritarianism, instinctively seeking to be self-determined, for along that route is survival. The other child may take tamely everything given out. The child with poor recall ability may be graded with a D, the one with better recall ability, an A. The relative potential worth may determine that the D child will someday be of great value to the society and that the A child of very little value.

Further, a child with excellent recall ability *and* high dynamic may be rebellious and so receive a low grade and yet this child is potentially the most valuable of the three.

Any society which remains indifferent to this by seeking to elevate the person of low creative-constructive worth above the person of high worth will find itself increasingly disadvantaged in competition with societies which do not remain indifferent to it. The reason for this is that when such practices are in vogue, they give the most education to those least able to use it, while they give the least education to those individuals of greatest potential value to the society. This creates an artificial and dull strata of the "educated" and invites totalitarianism by raising up those who are most affected by (amenable to) authority just because it is authority.

11

Games

A game is composed of freedom, barriers and purposes. That's easy enough to see.

What's trickier to see is how this comprises a triangle, like the ARC triangle. But wherever we look through life we find that these three points—freedom, barriers and purposes—are interdependent to some degree. It's one of the wildest-looking things a person ever studied.

One has to look it over and think of different examples to satisfy oneself that this relationship does exist, because it looks very illogical that if you increase barriers, you increase freedom and purposes—or if you increase freedom, you increase barriers and purposes. It just doesn't seem right at first look. One has to work with it a bit. It's not intuitive.

This triangle does, however, provide another way to explain why the idea of "Let children do anything they want, express themselves in any way," doesn't work. It's a total absence of barriers, so there's no triangle, no game. And they'll be very unhappy.

On the other hand, you can take a child and introduce one of these factors or another to help increase interest—you're simply making more of a game.

For example, purposes are very easily aligned and very easily handed out. They shouldn't be neglected. They help create games.

Children with games to play have purposes, barriers and freedoms and tend to be happier.

12 Imagination

A HIGHER FORM OF REASONING

One of the most important parts of the thinking process is imagination, which is actually a higher form of computation, or reasoning.

Imagination gives calculated and instinctive solutions for the future. If an imagination is dulled, one's computation is seriously handicapped. Imagination is a good thing, not a bad thing. With daydreaming, for instance, a person can convert a not-too-pleasant existence into something livable. Only with imagination can one postulate[1] future goals to attain.

If you take the word *imagination* apart, you will discover that it means merely the postulating of images or the assembly of perceptions into creations as you desire them.

Imagination is something one does of one's free will.

A person begins to take care of the future by imagining what is going to happen so as to be ready for it. He or she tries to foresee, through imagination, possible problems that will be met and to reach conclusions about them so that split-second action can take place when the actual problem is met. To accurately assess a situation it is necessary to be capable of imagining what is going to happen.

This is imagination in its simplest form. As imagination develops, it becomes more and more creative until finally it becomes the imagination of the greatest artist and thinker.

---

1 **postulate**: assume (something) to be true, real or necessary, especially as a basis for reasoning; put something forth (so as to exist); create. Also, the thing assumed to be true, the thing put forth.

IMAGINATION AND CHILDREN

The ideas children can come up with regarding how they ought to do something or what they ought to do about something are rather beautifully founded because they have very fine and imaginative minds but little data in them yet. And they have a fine time trying to measure up the real world—they are way out into the blue[2] with no trouble whatsoever!

Boy, I wish I could see in this country a few thousand artists whose imaginations were as unimpeded at twenty-five as they were at three, and with all the data too. You'd really start seeing something!

MATHEMATICS AND THE USE OF IMAGINATION

Imagination should be utilized in such a way as to bring it under the control, direction and self-discipline of the child. For instance, in mathematics it is necessary to observe and realize the existence of a problem, the factors of a problem and to combine these to predict an answer.

In life, it is imagination which delivers answers. If one cannot imagine, one cannot predict.

Of course, the factors of life are more complex than the factors of arithmetic, but they do not differ so far as mental functioning is concerned; there are simply many more of them. One can teach a child by rote that two plus two equals four, but the child cannot utilize purely rote data to resolve problems in the child's own existence. The ability to imagine the answer by recombining existing factors must be developed and disciplined.

Engineering schools are embarrassed when they turn out honors graduates who then fail in the reduction of practical problems to workable solutions. As precise a thing as mathematics yet requires in the good mathematician an enormous amount of imagination.

Symbols and figures, statistics and data in general serve only to assist the functioning of the mind in a solution of problems. These are at best crutches to

---

2 **into the blue**: at a very far distance or completely out of reach, out of sight, into the unknown.

be utilized by an active intelligence. The mind is always the servomechanism[3] of mathematics, a thing which even the better mathematicians are apt to overlook.

THE DISCIPLINE OF IMAGINATION

When we are trying to teach children, whether to be proficient in geometry or in handling their bodies, we must teach them as well to predict a future condition, state or circumstance; if they cannot predict a future, they cannot resolve problems.

Inhibition of the imagination of children directly results in the inhibition of their ability to resolve problems relating to their own environment and their own life. A child should be able to utilize this imagination and the imagination should be under the child's own discipline.

Thus, the discipline of the imagination is essential. In fact, the control and discipline of imagination and its employment for the artistic and practical gains of the individual would be the highest goal of an educational activity.

A good instructor realizes that it is the discipline by the student of the student's own mind which accrues to the student the benefits of education.

There have been great instructors in the past, great teachers who could lead their students forward by their own personal magnetism. Their effort was centered upon giving the students into their own hands, and this was accomplished by getting the students to desire to discipline themselves.

THE CREATION AND CONTROL OF IDEAS

Throughout the day and every day, children receive the message that things do not belong to them. If they're given a pair of shoes, they are informed that the shoes are not actually theirs by the first command from the parent that they take better care of them.

---

3   **servomechanism**: a mechanism that serves, services or aids something. Specifically, the human mind is a servomechanism to all mathematics because mathematics is something which humans use to solve problems: without the human mind mathematics is of no use.

In the case of nearly all children, even though they seem to have possessions, they themselves do not believe they actually own anything. Their bodies, their minds, their toys, their clothes, their habits, mannerisms, likes and dislikes, are all, to some degree, under the continuous influence of the surrounding physical world and other people.

There is a thing however, which a child can own and that is an idea which he or she alone creates.

In creating ideas which they then control, children discover first that they can own something, next that they can control something.

FREEDOM TO BE

By developing and utilizing imagination, children come into possession of themselves and are convinced that they are free to be something. The change with this realization is not an ultimate or absolute thing, for there is a gradient to everything and there are always new heights above any last plateau reached.

Nevertheless, it should be an objective of education to bring the imaginations of children under their own discipline and thereby increase their capability of being what they want to be, not what they are forced to be.

At the same time this will better render the child less reactive towards disciplinary actions undertaken for the child's benefit and towards educational measures which are provided for the child's future security. Acceptance of education on the part of the child will be found to replace what might have otherwise been resentment.

13 Validation

RECOGNIZING RIGHTNESS

An individual is basically and routinely good, capable of many actions and considerable power.

If you only look for things that are wrong and only recognize things that are wrong, then you will never be able to bring about improvement on a gradient because you won't think you have anything right to work with and build upon—it will all just look wrong to you.

One is *only* trying to find things wrong in order to increase things that are right, and that's very important.

If you keep on deleting or improving things that are wrong, all the while *maintaining* and *increasing* the things that are right, you eventually wind up with a very right person. You are trying to get a *right person*; therefore, if you don't continually encourage right things you never wind up with a right person.

The degree of "rightness" you have present must *exceed* the "wrongness" you are going to pick up. It's a proportional thing. If you want to pick up this little area of wrongness, you have to have rightnesses present which are big enough to engulf it.

RIGHT AND WRONG

Rightness and wrongness form a common source of argument and struggle.

They could be defined this way: A wrong action is wrong to the degree that it harms the greatest number of dynamics. And a right action is right to the degree that it benefits the greatest number of dynamics.

Many people think that an action is wrong simply because it is destructive. To them all destructive actions or omissions are wrong. This is not true. For an act of commission or omission to be wrong it must harm the greater number of dynamics. A failure to destroy can be, therefore, wrong. Assistance to something that would harm a greater number of dynamics can also be wrong. It is doubtful if you would think helping enslavers was right and equally doubtful if you would consider the destruction of a disease to be wrong.

"BEING RIGHT"

There is an irrationality about "being right" which explains why some people do very wrong things and insist they are doing right.

The answer lies in an impulse, inborn in everyone, to *try to be right.*

A person *tries* to be right and *fights* being wrong. One tries to be right *always,* right down to the last spark.

How, then, is one ever wrong? It is this way:

One does a wrong action, accidentally or through oversight. The wrongness of the action or inaction is then in conflict with one's necessity to be right. So one then may continue and repeat the wrong action to prove it is right.

So we are faced with the unlovely picture of asserted rightness in the face of flagrant wrongness.

Getting the offender to admit his or her wrongness is to court further degradation. Therefore, the purpose of punishment is defeated and punishment has minimal workability.

But by getting the offender off the compulsive repetition of the wrongness, one then cures it.

But how?

By rehabilitating the ability to be right!

This has limitless application—in training, in social skills, in marriage, in law, in life.

The student who can't learn, the worker who can't work, the boss who can't boss are all caught on one side of the right-wrong question. They are being completely one-sided. They are being "last-ditch-right." And opposing them, those who would teach them are fixed on the other side, "admit-you-are-wrong." And out of this we get not only no-change but actual degradation where admit-you-are-wrong "wins." But there are no wins in this imbalance, only loses for both.

You can be right. How? By getting another to explain how he or she is right—until he or she, being less defensive now, can take a less compulsive point of view. You don't have to agree with what they think. You only have to acknowledge what they say. And suddenly they *can* be right.

You can make yourself right, amongst other ways, by making others right enough to afford to change their minds.

IT'S WHAT YOU VALIDATE THAT COUNTS

If you believe in an individual as a sane and productive individual, they will be sane and productive—not because you coax them to but because you are just validating this. You are telling them by your actions and attitude that this is reality—their sanity and productivity.

Conversely, by validating an individual's weaknesses and shortcomings, you actually bring them into being and make the person weak and make them exhibit more and more shortcomings, making the person less and less strong.

It's what you validate that counts. The validation of difficulty will always result in the accomplishment of difficulty. The validation of ability will always accomplish ability.

ACKNOWLEDGING THE GOOD POINTS IN CHILDREN

It has been my observation that dignity and purpose are native to a child; being bad and out of control are not.

Children require understanding and assistance in controlling the environment around them, which is already too big, too strong, and is moving much too fast on them. They have to be set a good example of control and discipline.

This is not about heavy discipline. Consider this: How many people, when you were little, told you to be a good boy or a good girl, and then when you were a good boy or a good girl, never came back to you and said, "Thank you for being a good boy or a good girl"?

Have you noticed that often, if one is bad, it gets acknowledged and confirmed, but if one is good, it's sort of neglected?

By way of illustration, I've seen Blackfoot[1] Indians work this way. Blackfoot children tended to be very obedient, very cheerful. They were quite something to be around. The tribe was in connivance on every child. Every time a child, voluntarily or otherwise, would pick up a stick of wood to put it on the fire, they'd say, "Oh, what a good child." Or a child would go down to the brook intending some mischief and somebody would say, "Oh, you're going to get some water, what a good child." "You're helping your mother, what a good child." "You're being obedient. You're a good child."

It was the most fascinating thing you ever saw. This little boy will suddenly look so bewildered. He is caught off base. What he was actually intending to do was to blow up Bull Moose's tent! And somebody says, "Oh, you're taking that over to your father to give it to him. What a good child."

"I guess I was," says the child.

And when they were bad children, they ignored them. They just shut them off.

---

1 **Blackfoot**: a Native North American people living in the plains of the northwestern United States and Canada.

When you keep acknowledging the good points in children you keep making them happier, more able and more confident.

INVALIDATION

Invalidation is basically nonattention. Attention itself is quite important, for attention is necessary before an effect can be created.

WINS

It will be found that the way to success is paved with *wins*; therefore, when a student does something well, the student should be told so.

INTEREST

Every time you as an instructor get interested in students' *personal problems,* you are asking them to put up their personal problems for your inspection. Every time you get interested in their skill only, you are asking them to put up their skill for your interest.

In short, you get what you validate.

14 Control, Exchange and Discipline

GOOD CONTROL AND BAD CONTROL

The word "control," and control itself, have so often been so badly done that "control" is almost a curse word.

One way to view this subject is that there are two kinds of control. There's good control and there's bad control. The difference between them is certainty and uncertainty.

Bad control is uncertain, variable and unpredictable.

Good control is certain, positive, predictable, where there is clear knowledge of and agreement upon the goal to be attained.

Also good control sees one thing completed before the next task is asked for, whereas bad control looks like this: "Now, pick up that bunch of flowers—no, leave it there. Give me that book—put your things away. I told you to pick up the flowers!"

When we get a situation where tasks are not agreed upon, the goals are not agreed upon, the tasks are not completed, and so on, we get chaos and we get bad control.

Additionally, children who have no one in their vicinity to control them as much as they are controlling things will experience an imbalance of control and will get upset. The total absence of control could even be considered a sickness.

What does good control look like? Treating children in such a way that they can be in full possession of themselves at all times.

What sort of control do *you*, as an adult, want to experience? That's probably what good control looks like.

REWARDS AND PENALTIES

The whole decay of Western government is explained in this seemingly obvious law:

WHEN YOU REWARD DOWN STATISTICS AND PENALIZE UP STATISTICS, YOU GET DOWN STATISTICS.

If you reward nonproduction, you get nonproduction.

When you penalize production, you get nonproduction.

The welfare state can be defined as that state which rewards nonproduction at the expense of production. One could hardly be surprised if we all turned up at last slaves in a starved society because you cannot give more to the indigent than the society produces. When the society, by penalizing production, at last produces very little and yet has to feed very many, revolutions, confusion, political unrest and dark ages ensue.

There is nothing really wrong with socialism helping the needy. Sometimes it is vital. But it is a temporary solution, easily overdone.

No good worker *owes* their work. That's slavery.

One should be alert to rewarding production and penalizing nonproduction— and one should always measure that production by actual statistics, not rumor or personality or who knows who.

Specialize in and reward production, and everybody wins.

EXCHANGE

An inability to confront evil leads people into disregarding it or discounting it or not seeing it at all. Reversely, there can be a type of person who, like an old-time preacher, sees nothing but evil in everything, and possibly looking into his own heart for a model, believes all men are evil.

People, however, are basically good. When going on some evil course, they attempt to restrain themselves and will even cause themselves to collapse mentally or physically to prevent further harm.

Criminal actions can proceed, however, *unless checked* by more duress from outside the person not to do an evil act than they themselves have pressure from within to do it. Criminality is in most instances restrained by just such an imbalance of pressures.

Let's look for a moment at the simple mechanism of criminality.

Exchange is something for something.

Criminal exchange is nothing from the criminal for something from another. Whether theft or threat or fraud is used, the criminal thinking is to get something without putting out anything. An individual can be inadvertently coaxed into this kind of thinking by *permitting him or her to receive without contributing*.

Honesty is the road to sanity, health and happiness.

When you let somebody be dishonest, you are setting them up to become physically ill and unhappy. When you let a person give nothing for something, you are factually, if unintentionally, encouraging crime. Don't be surprised that welfare districts are full of robbery and murder. People there give nothing for something.

When *exchange* is out[1], the whole social fabric breaks down.

It is EXCHANGE which maintains a person's inflow and outflow and keeps the person extroverted and rational.

There are a number of ways these flows of exchange can be unbalanced.

---

1 **out**: not done, used or applied, or not done, used or applied in the correct way; things which should be there and aren't, or should be done and aren't.

It does not always go out the same as comes in. Equal amounts are no factor. Who can measure goodwill or friendship? Who can measure the reward of pride in doing a job well or praise? All these things are of different values to different people.

What can be plainly observed is that when a person becomes productive their morale improves.

Reversely, it should be equally plain that a person who produces nothing becomes mentally or physically ill—their *exchange* factor is out.

So when you reward a nonproducer you not only deprive the producers who are carrying all the workload, you also bring about a mental or physical collapse on the part of the nonproducer!

A lot of this exchange imbalance comes from the philosophy that a child should just be a child and not contribute anything or be permitted to contribute. It is this which first overwhelms the child with feelings of obligation to his or her parents and then bursts out as total revolt in the teens. Children who are permitted to contribute (not as a cute thing to do but actually) make noncontributing children of the same age look like raving maniacs!

When a person's exchange factor has gone awry, one should roll up one's sleeves and help them put it back to rights. At stake is their health and happiness.

And though thus easily remedied, by allowing children to actually contribute as a matter of routine, one can prevent the problem from arising in the first place.

ALLOWING CHILDREN TO WORK

The basic difficulty with all juvenile delinquency is the one-time apparently humane program of forbidding children to labor in any way. Doubtless it was once a fact that child labor was abused, that children were worked too hard, that their growths were stunted and that they were, in general, used[2]. Where there

---

2   The Industrial Revolution began in England in the latter half of the eighteenth century and then spread to the rest of Europe and America. Before reforms were enacted, many abuses occurred especially in England, including long hours of work, low wages, diseases caused by degraded working conditions, and forced child labor.

was an abuse of this matter, there was a public outcry against it, and legislation was enacted to prevent children from working. This legislation with all the good intention of the world is, however, directly responsible for juvenile delinquency.

Forbidding children to work, and particularly forbidding teenagers to make their own way in the world and earn their own money, creates a family difficulty so that it becomes almost impossible to raise a family. It also particularly creates a state of mind in teenagers that the world does not want them, and they have already lost the game before having begun it.

In modern society, the child who at three or four wants to contribute is discouraged and prevented from doing so. Then after being made idle until seven, eight or nine, the child is suddenly saddled with certain chores.

Now, this child is already educated into the fact that children must not work and so the idea of work is a sphere where they "know they don't belong," so they always feel uncomfortable in performing various activities.

Later on in the teens, they are actively prevented from getting the sort of a job which will permit them to buy the clothes and treats for their friends which they feel are demanded of them, and so they begin to feel they are not a part of the society. Not being part of the society, they are then against the society and desire nothing but destructive activities. Then when warped or pressed into some career, they are convinced that they are not really wanted and will come into difficulties regarding work.

Supportive of this is the fact that our greatest citizens worked usually when they were quite young. In the Anglo-American civilization the highest level of endeavor was achieved by children on farms who, from the age of twelve, had their own duties and a definite place in the world.

Children, in the main, are quite willing to work. Two-, three-, or four-year-old children are usually found haunting their parents, trying to help out with tools or dust rags. And the kind parents who are really fond of the children respond in the reasonable and long-ago normal manner of being patient enough to let them actually assist.

Children so permitted develop the idea that their presence and activity are desired and they quite calmly set about a career of accomplishment.

DISCIPLINE

There's nothing wrong with the discipline of a child so long as the discipline is leveled toward making the child more independent and self-determined—disapproving of the child being overly dependent, trying to build up the child's own ability to handle him- or herself, giving the child the encouragement or push necessary. In other words, you can safely apply penalty or loss to the child in order to encourage self-determinism and independence.

"I'm going to give you these four jobs to do. When you accomplish them, you will get a 'thank you.' But if you do not accomplish these..." (not being too critical and not being critical of the work when it's done either) "you will get a penalty." If you carry this along *without any temper or rancor on the child*, the first thing you know, the child starts to pick up some self-respect. The child has learned to handle him- or herself.

An out-of-control or destructive child must unfortunately be penalized to be educated into possession of him- or herself. Such a child should be given the stability of a penal code so that the child knows exactly where he or she stands. The code and the consequences of behavior must be invariable. This gives the child a certainty and a security.

By putting a bit of control in the environment, we have enough threat to restrain misbehavior. Discipline must exert just a shade more stress *against* misbehavior than the impulse for misbehavior does.

Children can be spoiled, but not by affection. The act of spoiling consists mainly in giving to them but never letting them own anything for themselves, or continually ordering them against their own decisions and then crossing the orders on them so that they have no certainty of the law under which they are operating.

A child who has been confused by conflicting orders and is in a sorry state can actually be brought into one of calmness by the establishment of a certainty such as a penal code. In other words, the child can be given certain tasks and full responsibility within those tasks and penalized *only* if the tasks are not done. Handled this way, children eventually rise up to handling themselves and should become calmer without becoming apathetic.

Reward a child when good, give the child specific rights and specific wrongs, and even a difficult child can improve.

15 Willingness

FORCING A CHILD TO LEARN

If you *make* a child take up learning a musical instrument (as parents and schools sometimes do), the child's ability to play that instrument is not likely to go very far. One would first have to consult with them as to what their ambitions are. They would eventually at least have to agree with the fact that it is a good thing to learn to play an instrument.

ALLOWING CHILDREN TO PURSUE INTERESTS

Once in a while we find a bad boy. He cannot be put in school and has to be sent to a military school. They are going to force him in order to change him. On the other hand, occasionally such a bad boy is sent to a school which simply thinks the best way to handle such cases is to find something in which he is interested and to allow him to do it. In one such case they took a boy with whom nobody got any results and said, "Isn't there anything you would like to do?" The boy said "No," and they answered, "Well, fuss around in the lab or grounds or something and someday you may make up your mind." The boy thought this over and decided that he wanted to be a chemist. Nobody ever sent him to a class and told him to crack a book, and nobody ever complained very much when he blew up something in the laboratory, and the next thing you knew the boy was an excellent chemist. Nobody interrupted his desire to be a chemist. Educationally this is a very interesting point.

Supposing we had only a few minutes as a football coach and we wanted to pick out who should comprise the first squad and quickly put them in good shape to win the big game. We would only have to ask this question: "Who here has desired to be a football player from the age of ten?" What about the little runt who has only been the water boy? He might turn out to be the best quarterback of them all because he *wanted* to be a football player. But the fellow who thought it was a good way to get a scholarship through school, make some money, or perhaps get lots of women because he knew that women gyrated around football players—this fellow will utterly destroy the team because he is unsupportable as a team member. His basic desire isn't there, so the willingness is missing.

CONSULTING A CHILD'S WILLINGNESS

It is interesting to watch a little girl, let's say, who has been around somebody who always consulted her but didn't take very good care of her as opposed to a girl who had the best of care but who never was consulted.

For instance, she is sitting on the floor playing with blocks and balls having a good time. Along comes her nurse, picks her up and takes her into the other room where she changes her diapers. The little girl screams bloody murder the whole way. She doesn't like it. The nurse keeps on doing this to her, placing her around, never consulting her willingness and the girl eventually grows up having to have *her* way.

WILLINGNESS AND CONTROL

There is the other side of this. You know a child is hungry and ought to eat. Little Bobby will eat if he is kept on some sort of routine. If supper is consistently at 6:00, he will get used to eating at 6:00. He finds out the food is there at 6:00 and so *he makes up his mind* to eat at 6:00. You provide the meal and he provides the willingness.

Then somebody says to him, "Hey, wouldn't you like to go into the other room and change your clothes?" and the answer is "No." You are making a horrible mistake if you proceed from that point on the basis of "Well, I'll give you a piece of candy," persuade, seduce, coax, etc. That doesn't really work. You take one of two courses. You either use good control with lots of good two-way communication, or you just let him grow. There is no other choice.

Kids don't like to be pulled around, handled roughly and not consulted. You can talk to children and if your ARC is good with them, you can get them to do all sorts of things. A little boy will touch the floor, touch his head, point you out and find the table. He will fool around for a while and after that you can just say

"Let's go and eat" and he will do it. He has found out that your orders are not necessarily going to override the totality of his willingness, so they are therefore not dangerous. You can confront him and he can confront you. Therefore you and he can do something.

A child might say something like "I want to stay up with you" and insist on doing so. But just letting children do what they are doing and not interfering with them and not controlling them in any way is not good for them.

However, children respond very readily to good control and communication—not persuasion but good communication. People often think that persuasion works with children. It's actually communication that does the trick.

You say to this little boy, "Well, it's time for you to go to bed now," and he says, "No." Don't stay on the subject. Leave it alone and just talk about something else. "What did you do today?" "Where?" "How?" "Oh, did you? Is that a fact?" "Well, how about going to bed?" and the answer will be "Okay."

Again, one doesn't have to use force or persuasion. *Communicate with a child, and control tends to follow as an inevitability*.

On the other hand, if you omit control from the beginning when bringing up children, those who look to you for a lot of their direction and control are cheated. They think you don't care about them.

However, as in the case with the playing of musical instruments, learning of languages or the arts and abilities, consult the child's *willingness*.

WILLINGNESS TO WRITE

I'm afraid the willingness to write is systematically destroyed in American universities. I have lectured on writing to Harvard University students and had them ask me how one develops style. I said that as far as style is concerned, one has to express what one wants to say and that is style. It is no more complicated than this. I suggested, just for fun, they try writing as Shakespeare or another literary figure. I then said to these writing students how to find out whether one had a style or not, or how to develop one: Just sit down and write a hundred thousand words.

The class fainted. One hundred thousand words! Nobody could write one hundred thousand words!

What was this all about?

Well, it appeared that here was a class of young writers that had been carefully trained to be very good in every line they wrote. That isn't how you write at all. You write! That is all you do. Write for lots of people about lots of things.

These students were looking for some magic sesame[1] and the professor there was carefully monitoring them on quality, quality, quality, correcting their ideas, punctuation marks, their schematics and so on—correct, correct, correct, chop, chop, chop. The final result of this sort of approach was a complete unwillingness to write.

You can also spoil someone's willingness to write by never giving them a response. If you are writing and writing but you know nobody is ever going to read any part of it, your willingness to do it will go by the boards eventually. This is because there is no communication involved. People get so bad about this that they cannot fill out reports. The Revenue Department deprives itself of billions of dollars of revenue every year, not because people are unwilling to pay their income tax, but because they know nobody is ever going to read any part of them.

It all comes back to consulting someone's willingness and then not destroying it when you have it.

WILLINGNESS TO DEMONSTRATE ABILITY

If you're going to increase somebody's ability, increase their willingness to demonstrate their ability.

It can be a dangerous thing to be able. It can get you into trouble. For example, you do a job well and people will keep you on it. All sorts of odd things can

---

1 **magic sesame**: a reference to the phrase "open sesame" to open the mouth of a magic cave used in the story "Ali Baba and the Forty Thieves" from the *Arabian Nights*.

occur along these lines. For a variety of reasons, a person is often gradually taught not to be superlative.

Willingness to demonstrate ability always accompanies the ability.

Now and then people surprise themselves half out of their own wits by failing to monitor their own ability. In a moment of great emergency they do something fantastic, like pick up and move a piano or an automobile or something. They'll say, "What did I do that for?" They are always able to do this, but they are not willing to. The motto of unwillingness is "it'd spoil the game."

And there's another consideration: It must appear difficult to others if one accomplishes something, since it is never appreciated unless it is difficult. The strong man in the circus must always grunt and groan while throwing a barbell up over his head even though it's made out of tin and sawdust. He'll grunt and groan and struggle, and so on.

And this is what a person is engaged in. "It's *hard* to do all this. It's *hard* to learn this. It's really something that should be appreciated. If I accomplish this, I'll really *be* something."

When people put up their own barriers for themselves to jump across, there obviously aren't enough of them in life.

Where there is an unwillingness to demonstrate ability, there must be some series of decisions in a person concerning the liabilities and consequences of the demonstration of ability which mount up to an unwillingness to demonstrate it.

Unless you change that willingness to perform, you change nothing.

16

Look, Learn, Practice

(Taken from *The Way to Happiness*® book,
precept *Be Competent*)

COMPETENCE

In an age of intricate equipment and high-speed machines and vehicles, one's survival and that of one's family and friends depends in no small measure upon the general competence of others.

In the marketplace, in the sciences, the humanities and in the government, incompetence can threaten the lives and future of the few or the many.

I am sure you can think of many examples of these things.

Man has always had an impulse to control his fate. Superstition, propitiation of the right gods, ritual dances before the hunt, can all be viewed as efforts, no matter how faint or unavailing, to control destiny.

It was not until he learned to think, to value knowledge and to apply it with competent skill, that he began to dominate his environment. The true "gift of heaven" may have been the potential to be competent.

In common pursuits and activities, Man respects skill and ability. These in a hero or athlete are almost worshiped.

The test of true competence is the end result.

To the degree that a man is competent, he survives. To the degree he is incompetent, he perishes.

Encourage the attainment of competence in any worthwhile pursuit. Compliment it and reward it whenever you find it.

Demand high performance standards. The test of a society is whether or not you, your family and friends can live in it safely.

The ingredients of competence include observation, study and practice.

LOOK

See what you see, not what someone tells you that you see.

What you observe is what *you* observe. Look at things and life and others directly, not through any cloud of prejudice, curtain of fear or the interpretation of another.

Instead of arguing with others, get them to look. The most flagrant lies can be punctured, the greatest pretenses can be exposed, the most intricate puzzles can resolve, the most remarkable revelations can occur simply by gently insisting that someone *look*.

When another finds things almost too confusing and difficult to bear, when his or her wits are going around and around, get the person to just stand back and look.

What they find is usually very obvious when they see it. Then they can go on and handle things. But if they don't see it themselves, observe it for themselves, it may have little reality for them and all the directives and orders and punishment in the world will not resolve their muddle.

One can indicate what direction to look and suggest that they do look: the conclusions are up to them.

A child or adult sees what he himself sees and that is reality for him.

True competence is based on one's own ability to observe. With that as reality, only then can one be deft and sure.

LEARN

Has there ever been an instance when another had some false data about you? Did it cause you trouble?

This can give you some idea of the havoc false data can raise.

You could also have some false data about another.

Separating the false from the true brings about understanding.

There is a lot of false data around. Evil-intentioned individuals manufacture it to serve their own purposes. Some of it comes from just plain ignorance of the facts. It can block the acceptance of true data.

The main process of learning consists of inspecting the available data, selecting the true from the false, the important from the unimportant and arriving thereby at conclusions one makes and can apply. If one does this, one is well on the way to being competent.

The test of any "truth" is whether it is true for *you*. If, when one has gotten the body of data, cleared up any misunderstood words in it and looked over the scene, it still doesn't seem true, then it isn't true so far as you are concerned. Reject it. And, if you like, carry it further and conclude what the truth is for *you*. After all, *you* are the one who is going to have to use it or not use it, think with it or not think with it. If one blindly accepts "facts" or "truths" just because he is told he must, "facts" and "truths" which do not seem true to one, or even false, the end result can be an unhappy one. That is the alley to the trash bin of incompetence.

Another part of learning entails simply committing things to memory—like the spelling of words, mathematical tables and formulas, the sequence of which buttons to push. But even in simple memorizing one has to know what the material is for and how and when to use it.

The process of learning is not just piling data on top of more data. It is one of obtaining new understandings and better ways to do things.

Those who get along in life never really stop studying and learning. The competent engineer keeps up with new ways; the good athlete continually reviews the progress of his sport; any professional keeps a stack of his texts to hand and consults them.

The new model eggbeater or washing machine, the latest year's car, all demand some study and learning before they can be competently operated. When people omit it, there are accidents in the kitchen and piles of bleeding wreckage on the highways.

It is a very arrogant fellow who thinks he has nothing further to learn in life. It is a dangerously blind one who cannot shed his prejudices and false data and supplant them with facts and truths that can more fittingly assist his own life and everyone else's.

There are ways to study so that one really learns and can use what one learns. In brief, it consists of having a teacher and/or texts that know what they are talking about; of clearing up every word one does not fully understand; of consulting other references and/or the scene of the subject; sorting out the false data one might already have; sifting the false from the true on the basis of what is now true for you. The end result will be certainty and potential competence. It can be, actually, a bright and rewarding experience. Not unlike climbing a treacherous mountain through brambles but coming out on top with a new view of the whole wide world.

A civilization, to survive, must nurture the habits and abilities to study in its schools. A school is not a place where one puts children to get them out from underfoot during the day. That would be far too expensive for just that. It is not a place where one manufactures parrots. School is where one should learn to study and where children can be prepared to come to grips with reality; learn to handle it with competence and be readied to take over tomorrow's world, the world where current adults will be in their later middle or old age.

The hardened criminal never learned to learn. Repeatedly the courts seek to teach him that if he commits the crime again he will go back to prison; most of them do the same crime again and go back to prison. Factually, criminals cause more and more laws to be passed: the decent citizen is the one that obeys laws;

the criminals, by definition, do not; criminals cannot learn. Not all the orders and directives and punishments and duress will work upon a being that does not know how to learn and cannot learn.

A characteristic of a government that has gone criminal—as has sometimes happened in history—is that its leaders cannot learn: all records and good sense may tell them that disaster follows oppression; yet it has taken a violent revolution to handle them or a World War II to get rid of a Hitler and those were very unhappy events for Mankind. Such did not learn. They reveled in false data. They refused all evidence and truth. They had to be blown away.

The insane cannot learn. Driven by hidden evil intentions or crushed beyond ability to reason, facts and truth and reality are far beyond them. They personify false data. They will not or cannot really perceive or learn.

A multitude of personal and social problems arise from the inability or refusal to learn.

The lives of some around you have gone off the rails because they do not know how to study, because they do not learn. You can probably think of some examples.

If one cannot get those around him to study and learn, one's own work can become much harder and even overloaded and one's own survival potential can be greatly reduced.

One can help others study and learn if only by putting in their reach the data they should have. One can help simply by acknowledging what they have learned. One can assist if only by appreciating any demonstrated increase in competence. If one likes, one can do more than that: another can be assisted by helping them—without disputes—sort out false data, by helping them find and clear up words they have not understood, by helping them find and handle the reasons they do not study and learn.

As life is largely trial and error, instead of coming down on somebody who makes a mistake, find out how come a mistake was made and see if the other can't learn something from it.

Now and then you may surprise yourself by untangling a person's life just by having gotten the person to study and learn. I am sure you can think of many ways. And I think you will find the gentler ones work best. The world is brutal enough already to people who can't learn.

PRACTICE

Learning bears fruit when it is applied. Wisdom, of course, can be pursued for its own sake: there is even a kind of beauty in it. But, truth told, one never really knows if he is wise or not until he sees the results of trying to apply it.

Any activity, skill or profession, ditch-digging, law, engineering, cooking or whatever, no matter how well studied, collides at last with the acid test: can one DO it? And that doing requires *practice*.

Movie stuntmen who don't practice first get hurt. So do housewives.

Safety is not really a popular subject. Because it is usually accompanied by "be careful" and "go slow," people can feel restraints are being put on them. But there is another approach: if one is really practiced, his skill and dexterity is such that he doesn't have to "be careful" or "go slow." Safe high speed of motion becomes possible only with practice.

One's skill and dexterity must be brought up to match the speed of the age one lives in. And that is done with practice.

One can train one's eyes, one's body, one's hands and feet until, with practice, they sort of "get to know." One no longer has to "think" to set up the stove or park the car: one just DOES it. In any activity, quite a bit of what passes for "talent" is really just *practice*.

Without working out each movement one makes to do something and then doing it over and over until one can get it done without even thinking about it and get it done with speed and accuracy, one can set the stage for accidents.

Statistics tend to bear out that the least practiced have the most accidents.

The same principle applies to crafts and professions which mainly use the mind. The lawyer who has not drill-drill-drilled on courtroom procedure may not have learned to shift his mental gears fast enough to counter new turns of a case and loses it. An undrilled new stockbroker could lose a fortune in minutes. A green salesman who has not rehearsed selling can starve for lack of sales. The right answer is to practice, practice and practice!

Sometimes one finds that what one has learned he cannot apply. If so, the faults lay with improper study or with the teacher or text. It is one thing to read the directions; it is sometimes another thing entirely to try to apply them.

Now and then, when one is getting nowhere with practice, one has to throw the book away and start from scratch. The field of movie sound recording has been like that: if one followed what recordist texts there have been, one couldn't get a bird song to sound any better than a foghorn—that is why you can't tell what the actors are saying in some movies. The good sound recordist had to work it all out for himself in order to do his job. But in the same field of the cinema there is a complete reverse of this: several texts on cine lighting are excellent: if followed exactly, one gets a beautiful scene.

It is regrettable, particularly in a high-speed technical society, that not all activities are adequately covered with understandable texts. But that should not stop one. When good texts exist, value them and study them well. Where they don't, assemble what data is available, study that and work the rest of it out.

But theory and data blossom only when applied and applied with practice.

One is at risk when those about one do not practice their skills until they can really DO them. There is a vast difference between "good enough" and professional skill and dexterity. The gap is bridged with *practice*.

Get people to look, study, work it out and then do it. And when they have it right, get them to practice, practice, practice until they can do it like a pro.

There is considerable joy in skill, dexterity and moving fast: it can only be done safely with practice. Trying to live in a high-speed world with low-speed people is not very safe.

PART THREE

Observations, Comments and Advice

On Interacting with Students

TRY TO TREAT OTHERS AS YOU WOULD WANT THEM TO TREAT YOU

(Excerpted from The Way to Happiness book, precept of the same name)

In all times and in most places, Mankind has looked up to and revered certain values. They are called the virtues. They have been attributed to wise men, holy men, saints and gods. They have made the difference between a barbarian and a cultured person, the difference between chaos and a decent society.

It doesn't absolutely require a heavenly mandate nor a tedious search through the thick tomes of the philosophers to discover what "good" is. A self-revelation can occur on the subject.

It can be worked out by almost any person.

If one were to think over how he or she would like to be treated by others, one would evolve the human virtues. Just figure out how you would want people to treat *you*.

You would possibly, first of all, want to be treated *justly*: you wouldn't want people lying about you or falsely or harshly condemning you. Right?

You would probably want your friends and companions to be *loyal:* you would not want them to betray you.

You could want to be treated with *good sportsmanship,* not hoodwinked nor tricked.

You would want people to be *fair* in their dealings with you. You would want them to be *honest* with you and not cheat you. Correct?

You might want to be treated *kindly* and without cruelty.

You would possibly want people to be *considerate* of your rights and feelings.

When you were down, you might like others to be *compassionate.*

Instead of blasting you, you would probably want others to exhibit *self-control.* Right?

If you had any defects or shortcomings, if you made a mistake, you might want people to be *tolerant,* not critical.

Rather than concentrating on censure and punishment, you would prefer people were *forgiving.* Correct?

You might want people to be *benevolent* toward you, not mean nor stingy.

Your possible desire would be for others to *believe in you,* not doubt you at every hand.

You would probably prefer to be given *respect,* not insulted.

Possibly you would want others to be *polite* to you and also treat you with *dignity.* Right?

You might like people to *admire* you.

When you did something for them you would possibly like people to *appreciate* you. Correct?

You would probably like others to be *friendly* toward you.

From some you might want *love.*

And above all, you wouldn't want these people just pretending these things, you would want them to be quite real in their attitudes and to be acting with *integrity.*

You could possibly think of others. And there are the precepts contained in this book [*The Way to Happiness*]. But above you would have worked out the summary of what are called the *virtues*.

It requires no great stretch of imagination for one to recognize that if he were to be treated that way regularly by others around him, his life would exist on a pleasant level. And it is doubtful if one would build up much animosity toward those who treated him in this fashion.

Now there is an interesting phenomenon at work in human relations. When one person yells at another, the other has an impulse to yell back. One is treated pretty much the way he treats others: one actually sets an example of how he should be treated. A is mean to B so B is mean to A. A is friendly to B so B is friendly to A. I am sure you have seen this at work continually. George hates all women so women tend to hate George. Carlos acts tough to everyone so others tend to act tough toward Carlos—and if they don't dare out in the open, they privately may nurse a hidden impulse to act very tough indeed toward Carlos if they ever get a chance.

In the unreal world of fiction and the motion pictures, one sees polite villains with unbelievably efficient gangs and lone heroes who are outright boors. Life really isn't like that: real villains are usually pretty crude people and their henchmen cruder; Napoleon and Hitler were betrayed right and left by their own people. Real heroes are the quietest-talking fellows you ever met and they are very polite to their friends.

When one is lucky enough to get to meet and talk to the men and women who are at the top of their professions, one is struck by an observation often made that they are just about the nicest people you ever met. That is one of the reasons they are at the top: they try, most of them, to treat others well. And those around them respond and tend to treat them well and even forgive their few shortcomings.

All right: one can work out for himself the human virtues just by recognizing how he himself would like to be treated. And from that, I think you will agree, one has settled any confusions as to what "good conduct" really is. It's a far cry from being inactive, sitting still with your hands in your lap and saying nothing. "Being good" can be a very active and powerful force.

There is little joy to be found in gloomy, restrained solemnity. When some of old made it seem that to practice virtue required a grim and dismal sort of life, they tended to infer that all pleasure came from being wicked: nothing could be further from the facts. Joy and pleasure do *not* come from immorality! Quite the reverse! Joy and pleasure arise only in honest hearts: the immoral lead unbelievably tragic lives filled with suffering and pain. The human virtues have little to do with gloominess. They are the bright face of life itself.

Now what do you suppose would happen if one were to try to treat those around him with

justness,
loyalty,
good sportsmanship,
fairness,
honesty,
kindness,
consideration,
compassion,
self-control,
tolerance,
forgivingness,
benevolence,
belief,
respect,
politeness,
dignity,
admiration,
appreciation,
friendliness,
love,
and did it with *integrity?*

It might take a while but don't you suppose that many others would then begin to try to treat one the same way?

Even allowing for the occasional lapses—the news that startles one half out of his wits, the burglar one has to bop on the head, the nut who is driving slow in the fast lane when one is late for work—it should be fairly visible that one would lift oneself to a new plane of human relations. One's survival potential would be considerably raised. And certainly one's life would be a happier one.

One *can* influence the conduct of others around him. If one is not like that already, it can be made much easier by just picking one virtue a day and specializing in it for that day. Doing that, they would all eventually be in.

Aside from personal benefit, one can take a hand, no matter how small, in beginning a new era for human relations.

The pebble, dropped in a pool, can make ripples to the furthest shore.

DEPORTMENT

Generally, the deportment of children most depends upon the attitude shown to them. If one is criticized by an adult, the others will criticize that child, or sometimes all will criticize the adult. If one shouts at them, they soon shout at each other. If one considers one of them stupid, the others soon pick it up. If they are treated with great politeness, they will be polite to each other.

HANDLING COMMUNICATION

The first entrance of threat or punishment or duress into communication will tend to cancel the communication line. One burst of anger, one note of annoyance in your voice, one miscalculation of effort, one slip, one failure to use good control, and to some degree you are diminished as a teacher.

On the other hand, if you do this well, you appear as a god to other people and to students. And you become unavoidable in what you say.

Of course, messing up a lesson, being yourself tired, being a little sloppy, losing your poise or something of that sort is remediable—as long as you are aware of the fact that the situation needs remedying!

THE PERSONAL TOUCH

It is the *personal touch*,
caring for the individual,
being considerate and helpful,
providing a warm, comforting, safe and cheerful atmosphere,
being understanding,
giving service with affinity, reality and communication,
respecting others,
observing good communication and agreed upon codes of conduct,
accepting and granting importance to another,
politeness and courtesy,
really wanting that person in front of you to win
and doing so unselfishly and without reserve.

Tolerance and friendliness of course do not mean lack of control and effectiveness, as these things are also part of the ingredients. The *scarce* commodity in the world today is tolerance!

DEPENDENCY VERSUS SELF-DETERMINISM

Dependency versus self-determinism.

This is the conflict of the child and the conflict of the student (not to mention the adult, the soldier, the president, the king!).

The way a person becomes less self-determined is by becoming dependent.

If a person has become dependent, he or she has essentially abandoned control of an area.

Mind you, dependency is not all bad. It could be considered that a fifty percent dependency would represent optimum action. Dependency uncontrolled, misunderstood or not understood by the individual, however, is thoroughly bad.

In trying to bring out full self-determinism in a student, dependency can be an enemy to that self-determinism.

If you take the level of determinism of individuals who have been corrected a great deal (the need for correction representing a dependency on another) and the level of determinism of individuals who haven't been corrected a great deal, you'll find out you have two entirely different levels.

You'll find that the individual who hasn't been corrected much will have a much higher level of self-determinism.

MAKING EDUCATION PLEASANT, UNHURRIED AND CASUAL

Almost all education has been hammered into the student as a "terribly important activity." Actually, it will be as much use to the student as it is considered casually.

This accounts, in some measure, for the tremendous difference in the attitude toward education of one trained by casual and interested tutors and one trained between the millstones of the public school system, with all the horrors of the examination for passing. And accounts for the complete failure, on the part of universities, to educate into existence a leadership class.

For example, consider the failure of child geniuses whose parents considered their careers so important that eventually their piano playing or painting will lose all lightness, creativity and joy. They will be as good, and as effective, as they can change their minds, change their thoughts, change their ideas. And one does not easily change one's thoughts and ideas in the face of such "importances."

The secret lies entirely in the fact that education is as effective as it is pleasant, unhurried, casual, and is as ineffective as it is stressed to be important.

THE DISCOVERY OF THE MISSING DATUM

A person's behavior is based on knowledge—or lack of it.

In children you may observe departures from what you would consider rational conduct. Don't just assign this to the idea that "He's just a child, after all." Children will figure things out as well as they can. If they have good data, they will act fairly rationally.

But sometimes they don't have much data and this results in peculiar solutions to problems. I ran into a little boy who had been punished, even though he was just trying to be helpful. He had buried the silver in the garden in nice rows because he wanted to grow more silver. This seemed like a perfectly good solution to him!

He then couldn't understand why he was being punished. Throughout all of this, nobody bothered to tell him that when you plant metal you don't get more metal. It was just a case of the child missing data.

When handling children, the discovery of the missing datum is very important.

When a child seems irrational, remember the degree to which children look out and see a wide, unknown world; major parts and portions of this world have simply not been identified for them.

"THIS IS A STEAM RADIATOR"

This brings a whole approach to view, and that is the identification of situations and objects on an educational level. What's wrong with this child? He or she doesn't have enough data and so doesn't understand. The remedy is to give the child more data. And don't give the child incorrect data, give the child the best data you can.

Ask the child to define objects and their uses. You will find the child has the strangest misconceptions of the surrounding world. So, what you are doing is educating the child; you are telling the child what the known world is about.

This is not about teaching spelling or something like that. This is about a type of education which is often not provided until you call it to people's attention.

"This is a steam radiator. The steam from this radiator comes from a furnace in the basement. Coal is put in the furnace and this heats up water. The water gets so hot it makes steam and that steam comes up in this steam radiator."

"Yeah, yeah. That's how that thing gets hot!"

"Right!"

You will be amazed how much you can accomplish by taking three-, four-, or five-year-old kids and educating them in this fashion.

You can educate children by just interesting them in the real world around them and properly defining things.

But we have to do that on a companionship basis, not on an authoritarian basis. If we are crushing this child with data all the time, the data will not be assimilated, it will just be parked over to the side unused, where unfortunately much education resides.

Again, you can straighten out an awful lot just on this level of providing the missing data. You're fixing up labels. You're helping a child straighten out the names of things and what they're for.

QUALIFYING DATA

It's good to keep in mind when giving children information that to say a thing is true, without qualifications, is in effect attempting to make a child accept your decision about a subject. Just look that over for a moment.

> "White is the combination of all colors."

> "Your grandmother has never seen Pike's Peak[1]."

Don't neglect the qualifying data:

> "The dictionary says that white is the combination of all colors."

> "Your grandmother told me she has never seen Pike's Peak."

In this way the child is allowed to make his or her own evaluation as to whether or not the dictionary is right, or as to whether or not Grandmother ever actually visited Pike's Peak. Dictionaries in some cases are not totally correct, and it might just be that Grandmother told you one thing, and gave someone else another version.

---

1 **Pike's Peak**: a prominent summit in the Rocky Mountains of Colorado, rising to a height of 14,115 feet.

18 Comments on Teaching Different Subjects

HANDWRITING

Children should learn two styles of writing, well and rapidly performed, susceptible to the easiest reading. Working for smooth and perfect formation of written letters first, the child should then study for rapidity without the formation suffering. Script and printing should probably be the minimum styles.

As the state of education and intelligence of a child is most often measured by the child's command of handwriting (and his or her spelling and grammar), an enormous amount of drilling can be done on this subject. Quantity of action rather than immediate perfection of action is most likely to result in rapid execution of the subject.

READING

A wide and varied ability to read, silently, aloud and accurately is most likely to produce an excellent command of grammar and spelling. It is quantity of easily read material which produces the result rather than minute perfection at the start. The keynote is familiarity gained by quantity rather than particular beginning accuracy.

Ability to read is directly proportional to the number of wins achieved and inversely proportional to the amount of correction. By choosing a slow gradient of texts from the most elementary to the more complex and using a quantitative approach, with a minimum of repetition of texts, a child should graduate easily from the Little Red Hen to Shakespeare without losing a wish to read.

Spelling and grammar can almost be neglected if a properly intense reading program is carried forward in sufficient quantity.

It might also be noted here that expressing one's thoughts and emotions without the benefit of extensive vocabulary is difficult. People with a small vocabulary of words are a sort of communication pauper. They often find themselves bankrupt in trying to say what they really mean, and this can add difficulty to their lives.

ARITHMETIC

A good and swift command of arithmetic should be considered a necessity. The formation of numbers, addition, subtraction, multiplication and division are the fundamentals children should be grounded in to the degree of instant response to elementary problems. Later this can branch out to angles and Euclidian Geometry. High number multiplication tables (above 12), squares and cube roots are probably best shelved in favor of an early acquaintance with algebra, log tables[1] and slide rules[2]. We are in a scientific era of mathematics where complex arithmetic has been exceeded by the demands of far more complex problems.

RESEARCH

The only salvation a child might have in the shifting patterns of our times is the ability to do quick studies of common subjects. It is not so much knowing where to look but *how* to look, and a familiarity with looking, that can bring the child to a state of rapid study ability.

---

1 **log table**: before the introduction of affordable handheld electronic calculators in the 1970s, tables of common logarithms were given in the back of math and science textbooks. (A *logarithm,* most simply, is how many times you need to multiply a number, say 10, by itself to get a number, say 1000. In this case, the logarithm is 3, because you have to multiply 10 by itself 3 times to get 1000. The log table would show the logarithm of 1000 as 3.)

2 **slide rule**: a mechanical ruler-like device used for multiplication, division and more complex functions before the introduction of affordable handheld electronic calculators at which time slide rules became largely obsolete. Prior to calculators, slide rules were used for over three hundred years in science and engineering. (The article from which this reference to log tables and slide rules was taken was written in 1961.)

It is a changing world. Many higher subjects are not stable for a year at a time. The student is only rescued by acquiring an ability to examine and know at great speed. This applies to the search for second-hand information, of course, but even more widely to search in the physical world. The ability to *examine* and *know* can greatly assist in the prevention of huge errors of judgment later in life.

A sample would be a daily assignment to report (orally) on the exact and somewhat complex status of something on a school's campus. Equally balanced should be posing problems and solving problems.

Example of a simple assignment: Go find a flower and count its petals and come back and tell me how many petals.

Example of a more complex assignment: Find a tree and a bush and find all the differences you can between them.

Example of posing a problem: Go out and find a problem in the front yard.

Later, when the child has a good command of reading, research assignments like the following could be done: How is steel made? When was the Tower of London built and why? How many kinds of cats are there and what are their differences? These would not be *after* a class study of steel, the Tower or cats. The assignment would be "out of the blue." The child must learn first to find sources.

The subject is further amplified by the addition of "suppositions." The child is told to find a tree and give some account of how he or she thinks it might have gotten there.

The keynote of all such training (in its early stages at least) is the abandonment of the idea that there are exact answers to all things. The world has very few exact answers. There are "agreed upon answers," "workable answers" and "policy answers." It is the sheerest folly to insist that *all* things have an exact answer.

If children are trained to believe that all answers are found in books and that all book answers are exact, their educational progress is stultified. As many of these beliefs can be counted on to change before they are 25, it is a disservice to freeze their thinking for the period during which they are being educated.

"Educational truths" as they apply in inexact subjects are created truths and are of finite duration. The child who is educated to *change* is never betrayed by his or her teacher.

The child's answer to the subject given for research is not criticized. Even if the flower has ten petals and the child has only counted five, that's the answer for current purposes. There should be no attempt to introduce accuracy in the child's observation. Accuracy will come providing inaccuracy in research is ignored. This is not true of arithmetic but it is in teaching research. A child will learn to observe accurately if not forced or challenged.

GEOGRAPHY

The ancient subject of geography has been divided into physical geography and political geography. Political geography embraces history and today even history is being rewritten. Thus a child may safely be educated into physical geography, while an historical or political geography taught would be of less use within the span of two decades—as has proved the case twice in this century.

Stars, planets, satellites, oceans, islands and continents should all be known well, a globe, books and maps being employed. The legends of these, including latitude and longitude, should be well understood.

Activities such as the building of the solar system or the layout of a continent in a sand box can make this a fascinating subject for young students.

ETHNOLOGY

Combined with geography, ethnology can be of interest even if it is less exact. A good text on the human races and their customs and habitats could be used with profit. This knowledge is useful, even though it is somewhat transient in character.

HISTORY

Any class in history for children should not be about making them parrot dates, for dates are nothing and easily forgotten. Rather, take periods in history and play upon the mind with a display of clothes, sports, children, kings, soldiers, politicians, sailors, boats, dogs, and, in short, the history of *people*, not events. Children are only interested in people, in children. That is all. A date is a date.

A VIEWPOINT ON THE TEACHING OF HISTORY

There are individuals, usually in the fields of the arts and philosophy, who postulate new realities for the social order. Social orders progress or decline in ratio to the number of new realities which are postulated for them. These postulates are made, usually, single-handedly by individuals of imagination.

For example, a man named Ibsen[3], by writing a few plays, wildly altered single-handedly the entire cultural aspect of Scandinavia within a few years.

Ideas and not battles mark the forward progress of humankind. Individuals, and not masses, form the culture of the race.

FOREIGN LANGUAGE

In the teaching of languages, let it first be said that four years of Spanish in high school and college are not likely to be worth a summer in Mexico.

Learning a vocabulary of five hundred words is not hard as long as one has no stumbling blocks which will convince one that speaking a foreign tongue is difficult. It would be of some interest to see the result if some school taught such a vocabulary to its students with the statement, "This is Spanish. Nobody else in school except you students will know what you are talking about if you talk in Spanish." Further, Spanish motion pictures with the English caption on the foot of the screen and with plain dialogue may teach more usable Spanish in an hour than a text will in a year.

In short, the *use* of language should be given attention. A foreign language should be learned for vocal use, mainly, and thoroughly or not at all. Learning monologues and skits can assist this. Large vocabularies rather than grammar

---

3 **Ibsen**: Henrik Johan Ibsen (1828–1906). Norwegian poet and playwright. He was one of the most controversial writers in Europe and jolted European drama into a concern for the problems of contemporary life.

should be stressed. Language phonograph systems may be procured and employed for this purpose. The ability to hear and understand would be followed by an ability to speak and be understood. Any such instruction should be intensely practical. A language is a communication mechanism, not a ritual.

STUDENT CONTRIBUTION IN ART AND LITERATURE STUDIES

It is particularly of the nature of fine arts that they permit viewers to contribute their own interpretations or originations to the scene—they do not exist simply to inform.

A work of fine art, such as a painting, a song, a poem or a non-fiction work, can elicit quite different emotional contributions from one member of an audience to the next, as they are left free to some degree to contribute meaning and emotion at their choice.

In fine arts, the viewer must supply something to make it complete. The response from the person viewing a work would be contribution, by which is meant the person is "adding to it." True art always elicits a contribution from those who view or hear or experience it.

Observations and Advice

THREE OBJECTIVES

In educating children one wants to keep in mind these objectives:

- help them build useful skills and abilities,
- make study and learning seem desirable, and
- open the world of knowledge to them.

THOROUGH COMMAND OF THE ELEMENTARY

Modern education sometimes neglects the firmness in which elementary subjects should be learned. For instance, many people currently have trouble with higher math and calculus only because they have a weak command of elementary arithmetic.

A thorough command of the elementary is what children should acquire. It is better to know important things extremely well than a host of things imperfectly. From this alone may be born a higher confidence in life.

LIFELONG LEARNING

Children should be unspoiled by prejudice and happy about learning.

As long as children and young men and women find pleasure in learning, they will continue learning throughout life—and upon that depends their happiness.

QUANTITATIVE APPROACH

It is true that a person can be quantitatively coaxed into doing something that he or she apparently couldn't do before.

EXTROVERSION AND LEARNING

It could be noted that earlier students did something that modern students don't do. You might think this concerns machines, electric lights and increasing entertainment available. It's simply this:

If you make people stay indoors when they should be outdoors, you will see a deterioration in their character.

The old-timer got outside. A person was able to live in the world. It consisted of fields and valleys and rivers and mountains. It consisted of rather boisterous weather and a lot of other things. People had solid objects around them. They had as much of the whole wide world as they could look at within a lot of walking in any direction. They had more world than the airline pilot who is skipping back and forth between London and New York. (That fellow doesn't have world, he has distances.) Therefore they could solve things, write things like the Constitution, the Declaration of Independence without a qualm. They could afford, when they did spend some time working on something, to really work at it, not work at working at it. And they could learn fast.

Now this might apply to education in a very interesting way. Suppose we had a classroom in which a child had to spend five, six, seven hours a day grinding away, grinding away and never got outside. We would suppose with that much study the child would learn something. But we see by experience that the more time he spends inside over a certain ratio the less he actually learns. There is something wrong here.

If you want children educated, you are going to have to furnish them an extroversion factor adequate to the introversion factor that happens in education. You have to give them enough time outside and under good control.

You could plan it so that everybody who was being educated had to have enough time doing athletics, for instance—good athletics with coaches, equipment and so on, not the standing around athletics, not the "if I have to put this sweatshirt on just one more time I will scream" sort of athletics. You could get them enough extroversion time outside, under good control, to balance their time inside, and thereby aid their learning.

Get them outside in some productive, organized activity and see if you don't notice an improvement in their character and an acceleration in their learning.

And specifically in the teaching of younger children, the periods of study should be brief but accurately timed and the recesses many.

EXERCISE

Health of a body requires some exercise. When a body is not exercised, it goes downhill, diet or no diet.

Exercise and correct diet keep a body going.

This applies especially to desk workers and students.

That's why one should be out there getting some air in the lungs and some limberness in the muscles for a short time each day.

MOVIES AND TELEVISION

The cinema has its points but they are all lazy points in that they do not stimulate the mind to visualize. The movie hands it all over and leaves nothing to be rationalized.

The influence of TV on the general crime rate around the world has been remarked upon many times, but the program material is what is being blamed, not that the child is being pinned motionless, and that is what's happening. I don't care if you showed them Little Orphan Annie sighing over the dog. Even if this is all there ever was on TV, and the child still sat in front of TV at an active time of life when they should be moving, you'll get a higher crime rate. All you've got to introduce is motionlessness; you'll get irrationality. Persuade someone to be totally motionless and to take it easy, and they get sick, their life goes wrong, they cease to be able to communicate.

Parents and Children

LOVE AND HELP CHILDREN

(Excerpted from *The Way to Happiness* book, precept of the same name)

Today's children will become tomorrow's civilization. Bringing a child into the world today is a little bit like dropping one into a tiger's cage. Children can't handle their environment and they have no real resources. They need love and help to make it.

It is a delicate problem to discuss. There are almost as many theories on how to raise a child or not raise him as there are parents. Yet if one does it wrong much grief can result and one may even complicate his or her own later years. Some try to raise children the way they were themselves raised, others attempt the exact opposite, many hold to an idea that children should just be let to grow on their own. None of these guarantee success.

The last method is based on a materialistic idea that the development of the child parallels the evolutionary history of the race; that in some magical way, unexplained, the "nerves" of the child will "ripen" as he or she grows older and the result will be a moral, well-behaving adult. Although the theory is disproven with ease—simply by noticing the large criminal population whose nerves somehow did not ripen—it is a lazy way to raise children and achieves some popularity. It doesn't take care of your civilization's future or your older years.

A child is a little bit like a blank slate. If you write the wrong things on it, it will say the wrong things. But, unlike a slate, a child can begin to do the writing: the child tends to write what has been written already. The problem is complicated by the fact that, while most children are capable of great decency, a few are born insane and, today, some are even born as drug addicts: but such cases are an unusual few.

It does no good just to try to "buy" the child with an overwhelm of toys and possessions or to smother and protect the child: the result can be pretty awful.

One has to make up his mind what he is trying to get the child to become: this is modified by several things: (a) what the child basically *can* become due to inherent make-up and potential; (b) what the child really wants to become; (c) what one wants the child to become; (d) the resources available. But remember that whatever these all add up to, the child will *not* survive well unless he or she eventually becomes self-reliant and *very* moral. Otherwise the end product is likely to be a liability to everyone including the child.

Whatever one's affection for the child, remember that the child cannot survive well in the long run if he or she does not have his or her feet put on the way to survival. It will be no accident if the child goes wrong: the contemporary society is tailor-made for a child's failure.

It will help enormously if you obtain a child's understanding of and agreement to follow the precepts contained in this book [*The Way to Happiness*].

What does have a workability is simply to try to be the child's friend. It is certainly true that a child needs friends. Try to find out what a child's problem really is and, without crushing their own solutions, try to help solve them. Observe them—and this applies even to babies. Listen to what children tell you about their lives. Let *them* help—if you don't, they become overwhelmed with a sense of obligation which they then must repress.

It will help the child enormously if you obtain understanding of and agreement to this way to happiness and get him or her to follow it. It could have an enormous effect on the child's survival—and yours.

A child factually does not do well without love. Most children have an abundance of it to return.

HONOR AND HELP YOUR PARENTS

(Excerpted from *The Way to Happiness* book, precept of the same name)

From a child's point of view, parents are sometimes hard to understand.

There are differences between generations. But truthfully, this is no barrier. When one is weak, it is a temptation to take refuge in subterfuges and lies: it is this which builds the wall.

Children *can* reconcile their differences with their parents. Before any shouting begins, one can at least try to talk it over quietly. If the child is frank and honest, there cannot help but be an appeal that will reach. It is often possible to attain a compromise where both sides now understand and can agree. It is not always easy to get along with others but one should try.

One cannot overlook the fact that almost always, parents are acting from a very strong desire to do what they believe to be best for the child.

Children are indebted to their parents for their upbringing—if the parents did so. While some parents are so fiercely independent that they will accept no return on the obligation, it is nevertheless true that there often comes a time when it is the turn of the younger generation to care for their parents.

In spite of all, one must remember that they are the only parents one has. And as such, no matter what, one should honor them and help them.

A CHILD'S AFFINITY FOR HIS OR HER PARENTS

There is apparently a natural affection from the child to his or her own particular parents. Now, I have no scientific proof for this. But observation, and just observation all by itself, demonstrates that children have a natural affection for their own particular parents.

When this is interrupted by somebody else or something else, a break of affinity occurs. In other words, a grandparent stepping in and jockeying the situation around until he or she is receiving the affection has actually had to break a natural affinity span between the child and parents.

Any family which permits to be in existence within it people or factors which will split up the natural affinity line between children and parents is asking for future wreckage as far as this child is concerned.

In addition, a child's reality consists largely of the relationship to his or her parents. It is interesting to note that any person who countermands the authority of a parent also undermines the independence of the child.

This is one to watch.

THE BIG GOAL

All data, to be of use to a student, must have a goal around which to align itself. In the case of a child, he or she already has a natural goal: the child wants to grow up. In fact, a child's wish to acquire skills, manners or anything else is based principally upon the desire to grow up.

Of course a child will have many minor goals: awards for doing a "good job," the admiration of fellows or adults, or any goal the child supposes valuable. But growing up is the big goal.

A society which makes the state of being a child a highly privileged one and demonstrates that growing up will result in a bad state of affairs is taking from the child the big goal, the natural goal, the one goal which would carry them forward.

You cannot overestimate the effect this has on a child. One will find in the society in which one lives that children who have received too large a bonus for being children are often those progressing least satisfactorily. They have been given importance, as children, way out of relationship to the importance given to adults in their lives. Being grown up should be demonstrated as quite an estate to be gained. Adults should enjoy themselves and their privileges in the sight of children. An adult should be something to be.

If little Willy suddenly runs into the room, knocks over a lamp, spills some sticky pineapple juice on a guest's suit, why, that's just fine. We pat little Willy on the head and we take him out and give him some more pineapple juice because he spilled his cup of it. Then we say, "Well, he's only a little child, he doesn't know any better." He takes a look at the adults around him and decides "I want to stay a kid because we get waited on, we get food, we get clothing and we have no responsibility whatsoever!" Little Willy has been robbed of his most important goal. Having been so handled, a child may (even unconsciously) want most desperately to remain a child.

In short, any system which gives children utter leeway in all their actions and coddles them in childhood will not help them become responsible adults.

In a child, the goal of most importance should be being grown up. Aligned in this fashion, a child will try to practice being grown up, and will mimic and learn with a great thirst.

MIMICRY AND MANNERS

A bulk of the learning done in a lifetime is through mimicry.

A parent may believe that children learn to use their napkin, knife and fork merely because they are told that if they don't use them properly, they will be spanked. By test, this inhibits the natural ability to mimic. The common result of this is to cause the child to revolt.

Evidence shows that if the child is permitted to observe, without coaching or coaxing, adults eating with good manners, the child, unless severely troubled, will struggle and fumble to mimic—and at last come up with manners. *Better* manners than those forced upon the child, providing the parents themselves know how to use table silver and napkins properly.

When the child, like those trained in the school of only-being-a-child-is-important, has lost any urge to be a grown-up, he or she avoids mimicry of grown-ups and mimics children. But the child mimics.

THE CHILD'S WILL

Parents rarely give children a chance. To get angry with a child who is angry is rather unfair.

The parent is a goliath compared with the child. The child acts in a "David" fashion in order to impress the giant and to hold his or her own against it, but the huge monster slaps back, saying, "Get mad at me, will you?" The child's will is quickly suppressed.

Perhaps Tommy will say, "I want to go swimming, Daddy."

The parent answers, "No, you can't go swimming today."

"But Jimmy Jones goes swimming all the time."

"I said you can't go swimming."

Tommy drops rapidly down the emotional tone scale through anger to tears and from there into apathy, saying, "I didn't want to go swimming anyway."

After this turn of events has happened a number of times, he no longer goes through anger or grief on his way down the emotions but drops instantly into apathy. Eventually when the subject of swimming is brought up he merely says that he doesn't like to go swimming, giving as an excuse that the water hurts his ears or eyes.

Simply put, parents would do well to treat the child as they would want to be treated, to give the child half a chance. And in particular, to avoid getting angry with a child who is angry.

THE TROUBLESOME CHILD

If you see some child who is making accidental breakages, odds and ends of disobediences, strange oversights, etc., you can be very well aware of the fact that here is a child that has been pretty badly badgered from some quarter or other.

Take, for example, a family that has a very bad or sick boy or girl. The parents may tell you they've never quarreled in the presence of this child; they've never punished this child; they've never upset anything.

Children can really get sick: things like scarlet fever and pneumonia and whooping cough and all the rest of these illnesses. You'll generally find that those periods of illness have been preceded by a very high emotional upset in the vicinity of that child.

Your first entering wedge in resolving such a situation is going to be in the direction of communication with the parents, and likely some education of the parents.

You may have to tell them and demonstrate to them, possibly using their own lives as examples, what happens when certain things happen to a child, how to better prevent the child from being upset and disturbed, and so on. You may have to show them the consequences of doing certain things to the child.

If any communication is going to be established between the parents and this disobedient and troublesome child, it will probably best be on the basis of "we have a life to live together so let's agree that you live with me in peace and I'll live with you in peace" or something like this. That may sound like a strange thing but children will listen to it.

"SPOILING" THE CHILD

When one talks about "a spoiled child," one has to really label and evaluate "what is a spoiled child?" before one can understand the act of spoiling children.

The way children are spoiled is to rob them of their independence of action, not by loving them or giving them things.

Children can be robbed of their independence of action in numerous ways. The first is to continually order them against their own decisions and then cross the orders so they have no certainty of the law under which they are operating. This includes inflicting punishment upon them when their own decisions lead them into trouble.

Another way to rob children of their independence is to continually inform them how everything is done for them, give them everything and then tell them how ungrateful they are. This is a method of buying them off so they don't dare act independently.

Another method is to work on the child on the basis of getting tired, discouraged, even ill whenever the child does anything wrong.

Lastly, there's depriving the child of pride of ownership. "Here are your nice new shoes, Johnny."

"Gee, that's fine. I think I'll go out and play with Rodger." And he puts on his new shoes.

"No, Johnny, those are your best shoes! You are to wear those only on Sunday."

In other words, he is deprived of his pride of ownership. He is deprived of his independence of action.

No child ever was spoiled by affection, by sympathy, by kindness, by understanding or even by indulgence. No, the fastest way to spoil children is not by loving them. It's by robbing them of their independence.

HOBBIES AND THE DEVELOPMENT OF SELF-DISCIPLINE

Self-disciplined children can handle their own bodies, and coordinate and handle themselves skillfully.

One cannot, however, talk to children about self-discipline because this is something that is a native and natural mechanism. It isn't something that is installed with a club the way so many people apparently believed in the past. It is something that comes about.

For example, a young boy learns that although he would like to go and eat dinner right now, if he writes just a few more lines in his notebook he will be finished and he won't have to worry about it later. His body indicates, "I'm hungry," but he doesn't immediately abandon his notebook. He's getting to a point where his thought and self- discipline are overcoming his physical needs. In other words, he has learned to use thought and reason to determine his own actions.

Not talking to children about self-discipline does not mean you can't help them with it. This is an important part of education, though not always recognized as such.

Let's say you have a young girl who is not yet able to control her body very well. One can help her by getting her interested in the real world through a hobby. But let *her* choose the hobby. And then let her show how proficient she can get at it. And you'll find out that something new is taking place. She is learning a skill.

This little girl, by practicing her hobby, is gaining precision control of her own body. It really doesn't matter what the hobby is. It doesn't have to be an academic subject, it can be walking tightropes or learning how to fry eggs or anything. The whole world isn't a bunch of selected subjects that somebody wrote down in a book. This is the business of living!

A child needs skills in the business of living and if they're interesting to the child, that's what you want.

As an example, take embroidery—teaching a little girl needlework. Now, this seems to be a far cry from anything being done much these days. I'm afraid the thing that is done in the home these days is teaching a little girl to look at a television set! But you actually can still teach a child needlework, embroidery, something like that. You have a concentration of the mind on the handling of the body.

One wants to educate and build children up to a point where they can handle their own bodies. When children get to a place where they can coordinate, where they can handle themselves skillfully, they have learned self-discipline.

Of interest is societies in which kids sit around rather sedately, practicing to be men, practicing to be women, and they're very happy. They're not constrained and nobody beats them. They are accepted members of the society. They have their work to do. They take pride in doing it. They're liable to certain clumsinesses and so forth occasionally, and they feel bitterly ashamed of themselves when they're guilty of such things.

They're pretty sedate. And the funny part of it is that if grown-ups didn't come in and stir up little babies—and their idea of play is practically throwing them up against the ceiling and a few other things like that—little kids would grow up with such an enormous sense of dignity that it's very interesting to watch.

And I've known kids in this society (in unusual homes, it's true) who grew up with a very great concept of their own personal worth and a feeling of great dignity.

It can have a simple start in getting a child interested in learning some skill, picking some hobby.

A CHILD'S PRIDE

It's important to give a child a feeling of pride in self and independence about a certain thing. There must be at least one thing in a child's life about which he or she has the only say-so.

This isn't hard to do, but first let's look at how *not* to do it.

Take a little boy who's walking down the street and sees in a window of musical instruments a beautiful accordion. He suddenly decides, "I want to play the accordion." He pleads and begs and does anything he can do until finally his parents break down and say, "Well, all right! We'll see if we can't give you some accordion lessons." So he acquires a small accordion, plays the thing, sees a teacher and finally learns to play something on it.

His family gradually realizes he can play the accordion. Mother says, "Why, there's Johnny playing on the accordion. Well, I always thought it was a good idea to start him on the accordion, and I'm glad I decided on that and got him to start it up." Suddenly, she's controlling Johnny's accordion playing! She says, "Well now, you must practice an hour and seventeen minutes every day; it says so right here in the book. You're not going to go out and play because you're going to stay in here and practice." "Now don't treat your accordion like that." "You hit the wrong note there, try it again." This is no longer Johnny's accordion and it's no longer Johnny's music. Johnny will probably take that accordion and junk it, to which Mother says, "Well, you know how flighty children are. They change their minds all the time."

The child selected something he wanted to do, then he was being forced to do it or was being interfered with in his doing it, and found out this was not an independent sphere of action after all. So he abandoned it.

You want to make sure children have reserved to themselves, alone and exclusively, at least one sphere of action in which they are completely independent, and in which they can do some shining—particularly one which includes physical skill. Because as children shine, their own idea of their own importance will increase.

VALUE OF A SANE HOME ENVIRONMENT

No happier kids have I ever seen than two kids of a couple of parents I met once. They were very happy, cheerful little kids. I was talking to the mother and they came in, they sat down quietly and they listened very alertly—and one was six and the other was eight—and they sat there, two little boys, very quiet and listening.

The mother told them, "You can go outside and play if you want to." And they said, "No, we'd rather sit here." Those two boys were as calm as can be.

Finally, experimentally I shoved over a gadget I thought they might be interested in, a ship telescope. I was thinking, of course, it would be pulled to pieces in the next five minutes. No, they found out how it was used and they found out how it was focused and a few minutes later were over at the window looking out and examining the neighborhood, using it the way it was supposed to be used. This fascinated me.

I said to the woman, "How do you and your husband get along?" And she said "Why, what do you mean? We get along all right."

"Well, what kind of a fellow is your husband?"

"Oh, he's a swell guy."

"What's he do?"

Well, he worked in shipping and he wasn't doing anything to be especially proud of but according to this woman, why, he was about the biggest shipping man that ever got to ship anything!

And I got more curious about this and I met the husband a day or so later and I said, "Say, what do you think about that wife of yours?"

He looked at me with great surprise, "But about the finest woman alive; you're not going to say anything against her, are you?"

I said, "No! Do you get along well with her?"

"Oh, sure. You know, I never really amounted to anything until I got married. And things are very nice."

I said, "What happens at night when you come home?"

"Oh, I don't know, eat supper and play cards with the wife and kids and maybe go for a drive, something like that."

And here were two very bright, alert, calm little kids. They never got into trouble in the neighborhood. Nobody questioned their reasoning, so they had no reason to question their own reasoning. And life was very beautiful all the way around. They will probably be very sane citizens and actually amount to something very fine in life.

Says a lot about how to have happy kids.

GIVING A CHILD "WINS"

Parents often try to lead their child too far. Nothing the child does anywhere is all right—it has always got to be better! Children are thus bred into an apathy, a recognition that they cannot do *anything* to please their parents.

This could be described as never giving or allowing the child a win—a *win* being simply *an instance of winning, a victory, a success.*

The parent says, "Talk better," "Get better educated," "Grow better," "Do this better," "Do that better." Parents often handle children beautifully on the whole except this one little fault, which if not spotted and isolated can actually make a child very unhappy. The fault is they lead, lead, lead the child.

Now, the idea of "letting a child be a child once in a while" is not the point here. Parents can let a child be as adult as the child wants to be, demand children be as much adult or as much children as they can be—that isn't the point. The point is simply this:

Give a child a win once in a while.

Here is this little boy growing up and all the time the parent is saying, "Well, yes, he's taken four steps but I want him taking five steps. He needs to be better, better, better." Well, once in a while, the parent could acknowledge the child's work in taking four steps.

The key is, in living with children, every now and then one should tell them to do something they *can* do, not something one *hopes* they can do.

One aspect of this concerns the parents' patience in letting the child work to the best of his or her ability. A small child will actually try to work well but will mess things up. If the parent is impatient and critical of these efforts all the time, the child, by the age of five or six, will have become somewhat disabused of the idea of working.

When adults forget that children are people too, things become unworkable.

A little girl comes in, maybe three or four years old, and mother is mopping the floor. The little girl takes a rag and bangs it into the wallpaper and so forth. The impatient mother says, "Get out of here now! You're messing things up." The patient mother shows her how to wring it out and guides her hand a bit on the floor, and lets her mop the floor a bit also. The girl comes up smiling. She thinks, "What do you know! I could really maybe be of some use some day!"

INTERRUPTIONS

Children, because they may bring danger upon themselves, find themselves continually interrupted in their physical actions. The child reaches for something and is turned away from it, not simply by words, but by being physically removed from the object or having the object removed. They are kept out of spaces they wish to enter by being pulled back. They are given one thing when they want another.

Thus, in their efforts to explore, obtain or get rid of things, children are continually having their self-determinism interrupted.

Such a child builds up a long string of experiences of interruption, not simply by speech but by barriers and obstacles. This can have the effect of inhibiting the child's power of decision, to say nothing of his power of speech and thought.

PURPOSE OF PLAY

A child's play is mock performance of future emergencies and efforts. In other words, the purpose of play is to practice the handling of self so that in the future, when those skills and coordinations are needed, they will be present.

FEED THEM AND PUT THEM TO BED

It is probably worth noting that some of the "play" you see children involved in is really just a kind of hysteria. A group of children are running around in the yard and all of a sudden they become very hysterical and their eyes start staring around and their voices go up to high C. Some people sit back and say, "Oh, look at the little children playing." No, they're going nuts!

These children are probably too tired and they're probably hungry; they're likely worn out. And the thing to do is to get them inside and calm them down—not just because you don't like to hear them yell, but because they're going to get worse and worse, and then somebody is going to get hurt.

If you take a child who is having a fight with some other child, you can fairly safely assume that they are either tired or hungry. Child is very cross, child is upset. Assume the child is tired or hungry or both.

Feed them and put them to bed.

21

For Parents

THE CHILD'S POINT OF VIEW

The main consideration in raising children is raising them in such a way that one doesn't have to control them, so that they will be in full possession of themselves at all times. Upon that depends a child's good behavior, health and sanity.

Children are, and let's not overlook the point, young men and women. A *child* is not a special species of animal distinct from humans. A child is a man or a woman who has not attained full growth.

Any law which applies to the behavior of men and women applies to children.

Let's just for the moment consider: How would any adult like to be pulled and hauled and ordered about and restrained from doing whatever one wanted to do? They would resent it. The only reason a child "doesn't" resent it is because the child is small. One would half murder somebody who treated them, an adult, with the orders, contradiction and disrespect given to the average child.

The child doesn't strike back because he or she isn't big enough. They get the floor muddy, interrupt the adult's nap, destroy the peace of the home instead. If the child had more equality with adults in the matter of rights, they'd not ask for this "revenge."

THE CHILD'S SELF-DETERMINISM

A child has a right to his or her self-determinism. One says that if children are not restrained from pulling things down on themselves, running into the road, etc., they will be hurt. Well, consider it like this: What are the adults doing to make that child live in rooms or an environment where the child *can* be hurt? The fault is the adult's, not the child's, if the child gets hurt or things get broken. The sweetness and love of a child is preserved only so long as the child can exert his or her own self-determinism. An adult interrupting that is, to a degree, interrupting the child's life.

THE CHILD'S POSSESSIONS

The way you make greedy or selfish children is to *make* them, against their will, give up their possessions to other children. If a child is permitted to grow amongst the society of children, they'll to some degree make a citizen out of the child about these things. He or she can go forth with these possesions, and can share them or otherwise. The child will find out how the world orients itself; that's something one's got to learn.

When a child is given something by an adult, it's the *child's*, not still the adult's.

Clothes, toys, books, what they've been given should remain under their exclusive control. So, the little boy tears up his shirt, wrecks his bed, breaks his fire engine. It's *none of the adult's business.*

How would you like to have somebody give you a Christmas present and then tell you, day after day thereafter, what you are to do with it and even punish you if you failed to care for it the way the donor thinks? You'd wreck that donor and ruin that present. You know you would.

Children wreck your nerves when you do it to them. That's revenge. They cry. They pester you. They break your things. They "accidentally" spill their milk. And they wreck *on purpose* the possession about which they are so often cautioned. Why? Because they are fighting for their own self-determinism, their own right to own and make their weight felt on their environment. This "possession" is another channel by which they can be controlled. So they have to fight the possession and the controller.

Freedom for the child means freedom for you. Abandoning the possessions of the child to their fate means eventual safety for the child's possessions.

What terrible willpower is demanded of a parent not to give constant streams of directions to a child! What agony to watch the child's possessions going to ruin! What upset to refuse to order the child's time and space!

But it has to be done if you want a well, a happy, a careful, a beautiful, an intelligent child.

TRYING TO MOLD, TRAIN OR CONTROL THE CHILD

In raising children, one can't "train" them into social animals. Some would say children begin by being more sociable, more dignified than their parents. In a relatively short time, if their self-determinism and willingness are constantly overridden or ignored, they revolt. This revolt can be intensified until they are a terror to have around. They will be noisy, thoughtless, careless of possessions, unclean—anything, in short, which will annoy you. Train them, control them, and you'll lose their love.

You've lost the child forever that you seek to control and own.

Your efforts to mold, train and control children in general react on them exactly like trying to hold this child on your lap.

Of course you will have difficulty if this child has already been trained, controlled, ordered about, denied their own possessions. In mid-flight, you change your tactics. You try to give them their freedom. They're so suspicious of you, they will have a terrible time trying to adjust. The transition period will be terrible. But at the end of it you'll have a well-ordered, well-trained, social child, thoughtful of you and, very important to you, a child who loves you.

CONTRIBUTION

Another thing is the matter of contribution. You have no right to deny your child the right to contribute.

People feel able and competent only so long as they are permitted to contribute as much or more than they have contributed to them.

People can over-contribute and feel secure in an environment. They feel insecure the moment they under-contribute, which is to say, give less than they receive. If you don't believe this, recall a time when everyone else brought something to the party but you didn't. How did you feel?

People will tend to revolt against and distrust any source which contributes to them more than they contribute to it.

Parents, naturally, contribute more to a child than the child contributes back. As soon as the child sees this, they become unhappy. They seek to raise their contribution level; failing, they get angry at the contributing source. They begin to detest their parents. The parents try to override this revolt by contributing more. The child revolts more.

It is a bad dwindling spiral because the end of it is that the child is likely to go into apathy.

You *must* let children contribute to you but you can't order them to contribute. You can't command a child to mow the grass and then think that's contribution. The child has to figure out what the contribution is and then give it. If the child hasn't selected it, it isn't the child's, but only more control.

A baby contributes by trying to make you smile. The baby will show off. A bit older, little Suzy will dance for you, bring you sticks, try to repeat your work motions to help you. If you don't accept those smiles, those dances, those sticks, those work motions in the spirit they are given, you have begun to interrupt the child's contribution. Now she will start to get anxious. She will do unthinking and strange things to your possessions in an effort to make them "better" for you. You scold her. That finishes her.

DATA AND SECURITY

Something else enters in here and that is data. How can children possibly know what to contribute to you or their family or home if they haven't any idea of the working principles on which it runs?

A family is a group with the common goal of group survival and advancement. Children not allowed to contribute or failing to understand the goals and working principles of family life are cast adrift from the family. They are shown they are not part of the family because they can't contribute. So they become "anti-family." They spill milk, annoy your guests and yell outside your window in "play." They'll even get sick just to make you work.

By being shown that they aren't powerful enough to contribute, a child is shown to be nothing.

You can do nothing more than accept the smiles, the dances, the sticks of the very young. But as soon as children can understand, they should be given the whole story of the family operation.

What is the source of their allowance? How come there is food? Clothes? A clean house? A car?

A parent works and for this gets money. The money, handed over at a store, buys food. A car is cared for because of money scarcity. A calm house and care of the parent means the parent works better and that means food and clothes and cars.

Education is necessary because one earns better after one has learned.

Play is necessary in order to give a reason for hard work.

Give them the whole picture. If a child has been revolting, he or she may keep right on revolting. But they'll eventually come around.

First of all, a child needs *security*. Part of that security is understanding. Part of it is a code of conduct which is invariable. What is against the law today can't be ignored tomorrow.

Adults have rights. The child needs to know this. A child has the goal of growing up. If an adult doesn't have more rights, why grow up?

Children have a duty toward their parents. They have to be able to take care of them; not an illusion that they are, but actually. And parents have to have patience to allow themselves to be cared for sloppily until by sheer experience itself—not by the parent's directions—the child learns to do it well.

You're well and enjoy life because you aren't *owned*. You *couldn't* enjoy life if you were shepherded and owned. You'd revolt. And if your revolt was quenched, you'd turn into a subversive. That's what you make out of your child when you own, manage and control him or her.

Potentially, parent, your child is saner than you are and the world is a lot brighter. A child's sense of values and reality are often much sharper than the adults around them. Don't dull them. And your child will be a fine, successful human being.

A good, stable adult with love and tolerance in their heart is about the best therapy a child can have.

22

Scales

Editor note: This chapter contains scales representing gradual states of change that were discovered by L. Ron Hubbard in his researches in the humanities. They are shared here for use, such as in observing signposts of student progress and growth. Unless otherwise stated, each is given with the lower states at the bottom and the higher states at the top.

EMOTIONAL TONE SCALE

enthusiasm

cheerfulness

conservatism

contented

boredom

antagonism

anger

fear

grief

apathy

A SCALE FROM HELP TO HAVINGNESS

havingness[1]

interest

communication

control

help

A SCALE OF DETERMINISM OR RESPONSIBILITY

pan-determinism[2]

self-determinism

other-determinism[3]

ETHICS, TECH, ADMIN

There is a cyclic sequence of things that must be applied and effective to have an organization and expansion:

1st ethics

2nd technology

3rd administration

With an underpinning of ethics, you can get technology (knowledge, how-to) of the activity known and used correctly. When you get the technology known and

---

1 **havingness**: owning, possessing, being capable of commanding, positioning, taking charge of objects, energies or spaces.

2 **pan-determinism**: willingness to determine the action of self and others; a wider determinism than self; not obsessive or compulsive control but the ability to see and be responsible for both sides.

3 **other-determinism:** a condition of having one's actions determined by someone or something other than oneself; assigning responsibility elsewhere.

used correctly, you can then establish the administration of the activity. Once all three are established, you have an organization and expansion.

Thus the sequence is ethics, technology, then administration.

If organization is unestablished, non-existent or chaotic, establish technology. If technology won't establish, establish ethics.

This can be found to apply to individuals, activities, groups and organizations.

And as things progress forward to higher levels of organization and productivity, it will be found to be cyclic: Ethics, tech, admin, ethics, tech, admin, ethics, tech, admin with each cycle operating at a higher level.

Appendix

Axioms on Education and Knowledge

Here is a collection of axioms referred to throughout the book, pulled together for easy reference.

- In education, a datum is as important as it contributes to the solution of problems.

- Problems and solutions are as important as they are related to survival.

- A datum is valid only when it can be sensed, measured or experienced.

- A foremost part of all education is the evaluating of the importance of data.

- Every datum is as valuable as it explains other data.

- A datum is important only in relationship to other data.

- A datum can only be evaluated in terms of data of comparable magnitude.

- A datum is as valuable as it has been evaluated.

- Arbitrary law is anything formulated and promulgated by reason of man's will, to be enforced by threat or punishment or merely disapprobation.

- Natural law is enforced by nature. Logic adapts decision and conduct to nature or adapts nature.

- The amount of arbitrary law existing in a society is a direct index to the inability of that society to be rational and to the irrationality of the members of that society.

- Only in the face of irrationality is force necessary.

- Authoritarianism is the introduction of arbitrary law where no natural law is known, yet maintaining that the arbitrary law is the natural law.

- It is a prime purpose of education to increase the self-determinism of the individual.

- It is a goal of education to sort the arbitrary from the natural.

- It is a principle of education to properly label that which is arbitrary and that which is natural.

- It is directly opposed to the best interests of education and a society to give force to any opinion of whatever kind and to force that opinion upon any student or individual.

- The maintenance of a high level of self-determinism is more important in educating than the maintenance of order.

Index

in ARC triangle, 59

Persuade someone to be totally motionless and to take it easy, and they get sick, their life goes wrong, they cease to be able to communicate, 121

threat or punishment or duress into communication will tend to cancel the communication line, 107

comparable magnitude

A datum can only be evaluated in terms of data of comparable magnitude, 36

competence, competent

Competence, 93

If one does this, one is well on the way to being competent, 95

not until he learned to think, to value knowledge and to apply it with competent skill, that man began to dominate his environment, 93

People feel able and competent only so long as they are permitted to contribute as much or more than they have contributed to them, 139

To the degree that a man is competent, he survives, 93

True competence is based on one's own ability to observe, 94

Confining a Child, 40

conflicting orders

A child who has been confused by conflicting orders and is in a sorry state can actually be brought into one of calmness by the establishment of a certainty such as a penal code, 85

conformity

Education designed to inhibit and restrain, to create conformity in the individual to the social order, has the unfortunate effect of reducing the individual in emotional tone, 8

consulting willingness

Consulting a Child's Willingness, 88

not consulting makes a child need to have her own way, 88

contribution

Contribution, 139

People feel able and competent only so long as they are permitted to contribute as much or more than they have contributed to them, 139

Student Contribution in Art and Literature Studies, 118

You must let children contribute to you but you can't order them to contribute, 140

control

children who have no one in their vicinity to control them as much as they are controlling things will experience an imbalance of control and will get upset, 79

Clothes, toys, books, what they've been given should remain under their exclusive control, 138

control and discipline of imagination and its employment for the artistic and practical gains of the individual would be the highest goal of an educational activity, 71

control is predictable change, 5

Good Control and Bad Control, 79

D

Data and Security, 140

Data Evaluation, 31

Environment and Data Weight, 19

remedy is to give the child more data, 110

sometimes they don't have much data and this results in peculiar solutions to problems, 110

The most serious hole in all contemporary education is its failure to recognize the importance of data weight, 31

When handling children, the discovery of the missing datum is very important, 110

You want data to get to people in such a way that they can get at it again, and if necessary, reevaluate it, 24

daydreaming

with daydreaming a person can convert a not-too-pleasant existence into something livable, 69

defining things

educate children by just interesting them in the real world around them and properly defining things, 111

delusion

child's real world as, 39

dependent

person becomes less self-determined by becoming dependent, 108

deportment of children

most depends upon the attitude shown to them, 107

deriving information

teach people to derive from the information we're teaching them the future information they will need, 25

destructive child

should be given the stability of a penal code so that the child knows exactly where he or she stands, 84

discipline

discipline by the student of the student's own mind accrues to the student the benefits of education, 71

Discipline of Imagination, 71

must exert just a shade more stress against misbehavior than the impulse for misbehavior does, 84

There's nothing wrong with the discipline of a child so long as the discipline is leveled toward making the child more independent and self-determined, 84

Discovery of the Missing Datum, 109

dishonest

When you let somebody be dishonest, you are setting them up to become physically ill and unhappy, 81

dogs

Human beings cannot be trained successfully like dogs, 7

drink knowledge at great gulps, 23

dynamics defined, 63

E

force

forcefully impressed data, 17

Forcing a Child to Learn, 87

nothing should be forced off on the student—nothing, 28

Only in the face of irrationality is force necessary, 32

The moment exterior force is applied, the student combats that force and is distracted from the principal purpose, in education, of learning, 23

foreign language

teaching, 117

freedoms

game is composed of freedom, barriers and purposes, 67

friend

Tolerance and friendliness of course do not mean lack of control and effectiveness, 108

What does have a workability is simply to try to be the child's friend, 124

G

game(s), 67

children with games to play have purposes, 67

composed of freedom, barriers and purposes, 67

geography

teaching, 116

goal

alignment with, 127

goal(s)

Good control is certain, positive, predictable, where there is clear knowledge of and agreement upon the goal to be attained, 79

Individuals are so composed as to overcome obstacles toward known goals and are not aided at all if you do all of the leading, 40

mind must be active, and it is active so long as it has goals, 24

natural goal: the child wants to grow up, 126

The pupil must have a sufficient goal so as to weight the data him- or herself, 31

good conduct

one can work out for himself the human virtues just by recognizing how he himself would like to be treated, 105

Good Control and Bad Control, 79

good grade

a measure of ability to receive and recall data without caviling at conclusions drawn by the instructor, 18

grade system

any school which teaches with threat and altitude by the examination and grade system, 14

grammar

Spelling and grammar can almost be neglected if a properly intense reading program is carried forward in sufficient quantity, 114

great gulps, drinking knowledge at, 23

interest(s)

A child needs skills in the business of living and if they're interesting to the child, that's what you want, 131

Allowing Children to Pursue Interests, 87

being allowed to fuss around in the lab, 87

You can educate children by just interesting them in the real world around them and properly defining things, 111

Interrelationship

of affinity, reality and communication, 59

interrupting a child's actions, 135

introversion

If you want children educated, you are going to have to furnish them an extroversion factor adequate to the introversion factor that happens in education, 120

invalidation

is basically nonattention, 77

irrational(ity)

All you've got to introduce is motionlessness; you'll get irrationality, 121

and arbitrary law, 32

force must be applied against the individual, but in such a way as to decrease the exhibition of the irrationality, 33

There is an irrationality about "being right" which explains why some people do very wrong things and insist they are doing right, 74

To make people irrational it is only necessary to interrupt their reasoning process and force arbitrary conclusions on them, 7

When a child seems irrational, remember the degree to which children look out and see a wide, unknown world; major parts and portions of this world have simply not been identified for them, 110

J

juvenile delinquency

a cause, 82

K

kingpin around an institution

is the person who is being educated, not the person who is doing the educating, 27

knowledge

An education which addresses equally each of these abilities in relation to knowledge, improving all and neglecting none, will improve the ability of the individual and his or her general capability in living, 47

A person's behavior is based on knowledge—or lack of it, 109

Axioms on Education and Knowledge, 149

Axioms on Knowledge, 36

definition, 43

S

U

V

W

IT'S HERE!

Applied Scholastics International® has teamed up with educational publisher Heron Books® to provide a collection of L. Ron Hubbard's writings on study, education and children—created specifically for educators! Now available in this newly released 5-book package!

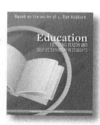

The Study Handbook
PRINCIPLES AND TECHNIQUES FOR EFFECTIVE LEARNING

For teens, young adults, teachers, tutors, parents—anyone concerned about real learning— this comprehensive book presents the basic principles of study and precise techniques for isolating and resolving any learning difficulties.

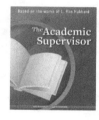

The Academic Supervisor

Once fully trained in study technology, training as an Academic Supervisor is necessary to successfully run a classroom of students learning independently. This is now easier than ever with this new book and its accompanying course.

Education
FOSTERING REASON & SELF-DETERMINISM IN STUDENTS

A comprehensive text on Hubbard's breakthrough insights into learning, education and children, including material from lectures and essays of the early 1950s, as powerful today as they were then—an absolute *must* for every educator.

Teaching
A NEW APPROACH

A simple, easy-to-read introduction to Hubbard's educational philosophy, including the role affinity, reality and communication play in understanding, basic educational principles, comments on teaching reading and research, and more.

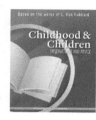

Childhood & Children
OBSERVATIONS AND ADVICE

A collection of essays introducing the most important principles an educator should know for success with children, including topics such as self-determinism, control, discipline, contribution, games and more.

heronbooks.com/aps-books

Printed in the USA
CPSIA information can be obtained
at www.ICGtesting.com
LVHW071346080124
768272LV00054B/1577